SPSS® Basics

Techniques for a First Course in Statistics

Zealure C. Holcomb

Pyrczak Publishing
P.O. Box 250430 • Glendale, CA 91225

Notice

SPSS is a registered trademark of SPSS, Inc. Screen images © by SPSS, Inc. and Microsoft Corporation used with permission.

This book is not approved nor sponsored by SPSS.

"Pyrczak Publishing" is an imprint of Fred Pyrczak, Publisher, A California Corporation.

Although the author and publisher have made every effort to ensure the accuracy and completeness of information contained in this book, we assume no responsibility for errors, inaccuracies, omissions, or any inconsistency herein. Any slights of people, places, or organizations are unintentional.

Project Director: Monica Lopez.

Cover design by Robert Kibler and Larry Nichols.

Technical assistance provided by Cheryl Alcorn, Tamara L. Caldwell, and Jack Petit.

Editorial assistance provided by Randall R. Bruce, Karen M. Disner, Jennifer Kelly, Brenda Koplin, Erica Simmons, and Sharon Young.

Printed in the United States of America by Malloy, Inc.

ISBN 1-884585-67-1

Preface

SPSS is a powerful, complex computer program for statistical analysis. Its complexity allows experienced researchers to perform both simple and complex statistical procedures. Unfortunately, for students just beginning their study of statistics, its complexity can cause confusion. This book is designed to overcome this problem by focusing on just the very basic statistics typically covered in a first course on statistics.

Sequence of This Book

The sequence of this book follows the traditional sequence of most introductory statistics textbooks. For instance, how to build a histogram using SPSS is introduced early in this book, as it is in introductory statistics textbooks, while how to produce a scattergram is introduced much later. This organization differs from that of other books on how to use SPSS. For instance, other books might show how to produce a variety of different types of statistical figures (i.e., graphs and charts) in a single chapter, even though some figures are taught near the beginning of a statistics course, while other figures are typically taught weeks later.

The sequence of this book makes it easy for students to start using SPSS right away in their statistics courses and follow along using SPSS as they learn new concepts and procedures for which computational output is needed.

Contents of Individual Chapters

Chapter 1 describes the traditional levels of measurement with terminology typically used in statistics textbooks. It also introduces the terminology used by SPSS, which differs slightly from the conventional terminology. Knowledge of levels of measurement is important because the level at which a variable is measured helps to determine which statistical procedures are appropriate.

Chapter 2 shows students how to enter the data for a variable into SPSS and save it as an SPSS data file.

Each of the remaining chapters deals with a limited number of statistical procedures. For each, there are brief definitions, followed by information on when to use the procedure(s). Next, each procedure is described step by step with a profusion of screen shots containing superimposed arrows that describe exactly what to do to get the desired SPSS output. Finally, each of these chapters ends with directions and examples that show how to format and report the unformatted SPSS output so that it is consistent with the guidelines in the *Publication Manual of the American Psychological Association*, which is the most widely used style manual in the behavioral and social sciences.

Versions of SPSS

This book was written using the student version of SPSS 13.0 for Windows. Periodically, SPSS issues new versions of its software products. While the new versions have enhanced features at the advanced level, changes at the basic level are typically negligible. Nevertheless, if you are using a version other than 13.0, you may notice some minor discrepancies from what you will find in this book.

Acknowledgments

I am grateful to Dr. Matthew Giblin of Southern Illinois University, Carbondale; Dr. Deborah M. Oh of California State University, Los Angeles; and Dr. Richard Rasor of American River College for their many useful suggestions for improving the first draft of this book.

Concluding Comments

I encourage you to share with me your criticisms of this book. You can communicate with me via my publisher. The mailing address is shown on the title page of this book. Also, you can send e-mails to me in care of the publisher at Info@Pyrczak.com.

Zealure C. Holcomb

Contents

Notes:

Detailed Contents

Notes:

Learning Objectives

5. Identify the mode in a frequency distribution.

6. Present the mean and median in a research report.

    a. Select the appropriate symbol for the mean.

    b. Determine the number of decimal places to use when reporting the mean and median.

1. Review the definition of the mean.

2. Define the standard deviation.

3. Identify when to use the mean and standard deviation.

4. Identify when to use the median and interquartile range.

5. Enter data consisting of codes for group membership and scores for a scale variable.

6. Identify independent and dependent variables for analysis by SPSS.

7. Calculate the means and standard deviations separately for each group.

8. Present means and standard deviations in a research report.

    a. Present means and standard deviations within a sentence.

    b. Present means and standard deviations in a statistical table.

1. Define the terms "*z*-score," "standard score," and "standardized values."

2. Calculate *z*-scores for individuals in a group.

3. Interpret *z*-scores.

4. Identify uses for *z*-scores.

1. Define the term "scattergram."

2. Identify when to use a scattergram.

3. Create a scattergram using SPSS.

4. Interpret a scattergram in terms of:

    a. strength,

    b. direction, and

    c. linearity.

5. Format a scattergram for presentation in a research report.

1. Define the term "correlation coefficient."

2. Identify when to use the Pearson *r*.

3. Identify when to use Spearman's *rho*.

4. Interpret a correlation coefficient in terms of its strength and direction.

5. Present a correlation coefficient in a research report.

1. Identify purpose of the *t* test for a single sample mean.

2. Conduct a *t* test to determine the significance of the difference between a single sample mean and a test value
    (i.e., a known value or hypothetical value).

3. Interpret the results of the *t* test in terms of the null hypothesis and statistical significance.

4. Present the results of the *t* test in a research report.

Notes:

Chapter 1

Levels of Measurement in SPSS

Learning objectives:
1. Identify the major steps in conducting research.
2. Define traditional levels of measurement.
3. Define levels of measurement used by SPSS.
4. Compare traditional levels with SPSS levels.
5. Define the term *variable*.
6. Classify variables as *categorical* or *scale*.
7. Classify variables as *nominal*, *ordinal*, or *scale*.

Introductory Comment

The terminology on levels of measurement presented in this chapter should be mastered early because the proper identification of levels is essential for identifying the appropriate statistical methods to use when analyzing a given set of data.

Levels of Measurement in Research

Research is the process of *systematically collecting*, *analyzing*, and *interpreting* information. The information obtained from this process is called *data*. More specifically:

1. Researchers *collect data* using a variety of tools such as:

   a. paper-and-pencil achievement and aptitude tests,
   b. paper-and-pencil personality and attitude scales as well as questionnaires,
   c. direct observation of overt physical behaviors with checklists,
   d. structured interviews with fixed choices for respondents to choose from, and
   e. semistructured interviews with open-ended questions.

2. Data collection is *systematic* when researchers plan in advance *what* to observe, *whom* to observe, *when* to observe, and *how* to observe. For instance, a researcher might decide to observe the self-esteem of low-achieving students near the end of sixth grade using a previously validated self-esteem scale consisting of a set of statements to which the students respond with choices from Strongly Agree to Strongly Disagree. The scores students obtain on the scale are the *data*. Researchers also plan in advance *how to analyze* the data. For this example involving low-achieving students, the researcher has planned:

   a. *What to observe*: self-esteem.

b. *Whom to observe*: low-achieving students.

c. *When to observe*: near the end of sixth grade.

d. *How to observe*: previously validated self-esteem scale.

e. *How to analyze*: calculate a mean using SPSS.

3. Researchers *analyze data* using a wide variety of statistical methods. The method(s) a researcher chooses for analyzing a given set of data depends primarily on two considerations:

a. The purposes of the research. For instance, describing the self-esteem of one group of students will involve different statistical methods from statistical methods for comparing the self-esteem of two or more groups of students.

b. The characteristics of the data. One of the most important characteristics of a set of data is its *level of measurement*,[1] which is the primary topic of this chapter. Knowing the level of measurement is essential for selecting the correct statistical methods.

4. Researchers *interpret* the data they collect in light of the statistical results as well as in light of the strengths and weaknesses of the research methodology they employed. For instance, a researcher will have less confidence in the validity of an average score for a group if a biased sample instead of a random sample is studied.

Traditional Levels of Measurement

As you know from point 3.b. above, choosing appropriate statistical methods depends in part on the levels of measurement employed to collect the data, a topic that will be discussed at various points throughout this book. The traditional terms for levels of measurement used by most writers of statistics textbooks are slightly different from those used by SPSS. First, consider the traditional levels. The first level is the *nominal level of measurement*.

Nominal Level of Measurement

Data collected at the nominal level consist of word *names* (not numbers) that put research participants[2] into discrete categories. For instance, data collected on "political affiliation" are often cast in terms of these names: Republican–Democrat–other. Other examples at the nominal level are gender (male–female) and country of origin (e.g., USA–Canada–Mexico, etc.).

Note that nominal data do not indicate who is higher or lower than any other participant, at least not in a way on which all researchers could agree. For instance, researchers could not all agree that Republican is higher (i.e., better) than Democrat. (In contrast, in the next level of measurement, participants are ordered from high to low.)

---

[1] Many writers use the term "scales of measurement" synonymously with the term "levels of measurement."

[2] The traditional term for individuals who are studied is *subjects*. In recent decades, the term *participants* has for the most part replaced the term *subjects* in published research in the social and behavioral sciences. The term *participants* implies that the individuals freely consented to participate in the research and are not objects (i.e., subjects) studied without consent. Thus, the term *participants* instead of *subjects* is used throughout this book.

Ordinal Level of Measurement

At the *ordinal level*, research participants are put in order from high to low. For instance, those who have advanced college degrees belong to a category that is higher than the category for participants who have only a bachelor's degree. Those with a bachelor's degree are higher than college dropouts, and so on.

Ordinal data can be obtained by ranking (e.g., giving a rank of "1" to the participant who has the largest amount of some characteristic, a rank of "2" to the participant with the second largest amount, and so on). For instance, each participant who has an advanced college degree could be given a rank of 1; each with only a bachelor's degree could be given a rank of 2; each who is a college dropout could be given a rank of 3; and so on.

Consider another example: Suppose students in a classroom were ranked according to their height. A rank of "1" would identify the tallest student, a rank of "2" would indicate the next tallest, and so on. Notice that these ranks do *not* indicate how much taller the first student is than the next. The first student might be only an inch taller than the second one, or he or she might be a foot taller than the second one. The failure of ordinal data to indicate how much more of a characteristic one participant has than another participant is a weakness of ordinal data.

Because of this weakness (failure to indicate the *amount* of difference among participants), researchers often avoid measuring at the ordinal level whenever it is possible to measure a given variable at one of the two following levels.

Interval Level of Measurement

At the *interval level*, each score point is equally distant from each other score point (unlike ranks; see above). For instance, almost all researchers assume that multiple-choice measures (e.g., achievement tests, personality scales) yield scores with equal intervals among them. Consider a multiple-choice intelligence test. Psychological researchers usually assume that the IQ scores are at equal intervals such that the difference in intelligence between IQs of 100 and 110 equals the same amount of difference in intelligence as the difference between IQs of 110 and 120.

While the interval level has equal intervals among the scores, it does not have an absolute or "real" zero point. For instance, suppose an examinee marked all the items on an IQ test incorrectly, obtaining a score of zero. This does not mean that the examinee is devoid of all intelligence because the zero point is arbitrary. It is arbitrary because intelligence tests contain only a sample of behaviors that indicate intelligence. Such tests do not include the lowest levels of intelligent human behavior (e.g., ability to blink at the sun). Because they do not do so, the tests are unable to identify individuals who are truly at zero.

Ratio Level of Measurement

At the *ratio level*, each score point is (or is assumed to be) equally distant from each other score point, which is also true of the interval level discussed immediately above. However, at the ratio level, researchers can identify the absolute zero. The most common examples are in the physical sciences. For instance, consider the characteristic called *weight*. When an accurate scale indicates that the weight equals zero, this means that there is, in real terms, no weight (i.e., there is nothing on the scale).

To mathematicians, there are instances in which the difference between the interval and ratio levels is important. For most applied researcher problems, however, whether the data are interval or ratio has no bearing on how the data are analyzed. In SPSS, this fact is acknowledged by not distinguishing between the interval and ratio levels when using the SPSS program (see *Scale Level* below).

SPSS Levels of Measurement

Students who are using a traditional statistics textbook in conjunction with this book should already be familiar with the traditional levels discussed above. However, when learning to use SPSS, it is important to also know the terminology used by SPSS for levels of measurement. The SPSS levels are as follows.

Categorical Level: Nominal and Ordinal

In SPSS, the terms *nominal* and *ordinal* are used as defined earlier in this chapter. Note that SPSS publications also use the term *categorical*, which refers to both the nominal and ordinal levels.

Scale Level: Interval and Ratio

SPSS uses the term *scale* to refer to both the interval and ratio levels of measurement, as defined earlier in this chapter. Put another way, users of SPSS do not need to distinguish between the traditional interval and ratio levels.

Comparison of Traditional and SPSS Levels of Measurement

Table 1.1 on the next page summarizes and compares the two classification systems: the traditional and the one used by SPSS. Note that the major difference is that SPSS uses the general term *scale* to refer to both the interval and ratio levels.

Table 1.1

Summary and Comparison of Traditional and SPSS Terminology for Levels of Measurement

Traditional	SPSS	Definition	Example
	Categorical	General term for nominal and ordinal	
Nominal		Naming data	Gender: male–female
Ordinal		Ordered data	Highest degree earned
	Scale	General term for interval and ratio	
Interval		Equal intervals without absolute zero	Multiple-choice scores
Ratio		Equal intervals with absolute zero	Weight (in pounds)

Variables in SPSS

Researchers use the technical term *variable* to stand for a trait or characteristic that varies among the participants in a study.[3] In SPSS, you will be identifying variables as either *nominal variables*, *ordinal variables*, or *scale variables* (see Table 1.1 above).

Exercise for Chapter 1

1. In addition to planning what, whom, when, and how to observe, what else do researchers plan before conducting their research?

2. What are the two primary considerations researchers use when choosing statistical methods for analyzing a given set of data?

3. Number-right scores on a multiple-choice math test are at what level of measurement?

   a. Nominal.   b. Ordinal.   c. Interval.   d. Ratio.

4. Religious affiliation measured by grouping individuals into categories such as Protestant, Catholic, and so on is at what level of measurement?

   a. Nominal.   b. Ordinal.   c. Interval.   d. Ratio.

5. Researchers often avoid measuring at what level of measurement when they can measure a given variable at a higher level?

   a. Nominal.   b. Ordinal.   c. Interval.   d. Ratio.

---

[3] For instance, gender is a *variable*, with participants in research *varying* (i.e., being different from each other) because some are male and some are female. Another example: If a researcher measures knowledge of American geography with a 20-item true–false test, the examinees can *vary* in their scores from zero correct to 20 correct. In this case, geography knowledge is a *variable*.

6. Consider a variable that has an absolute zero (such as time elapsed since an event) and has equal intervals. In SPSS, this variable is categorized as being which of the following?

a. Nominal.   b. Ordinal.   c. Scale.

7. Scores on a multiple-choice personality scale that measures depression are at what level of measurement in SPSS?

a. Nominal.   b. Ordinal.   c. Scale.

8. A researcher classified participants according to the states (e.g., New York, Texas) in which they were born. The researcher has measured at what SPSS level?

a. Nominal.   b. Ordinal.   c. Scale.

9. A researcher rank-orders participants according to their weight, giving the heaviest participant a rank of 1, the next heaviest a rank of 2, and so on. He or she has measured at what SPSS level?

a. Nominal.   b. Ordinal.   c. Scale.

10. A researcher measured a variable at the interval level. He or she has measured at which SPSS level?

a. Nominal.   b. Ordinal.   c. Scale.

11. In SPSS publications, what general term is used to refer to both *nominal* and *ordinal* data?

12. What is the technical term that researchers use to stand for a trait or characteristic that varies among the participants in a study?

Chapter 2

Entering and Saving a
Set of Scores (*Scale* Variable)

> ***Learning objectives*:**
> 1. Start SPSS.
> 2. Distinguish between *numeric data* and *string data*.
> 3. Distinguish between "Variable View" and "Data View" in the Data Editor.
> 4. Name a variable.
> 5. Give the variable a label.
> 6. Enter scores for a *scale variable* (i.e., ratio or interval).
> 7. Save the data file, and close SPSS.

Introductory Comment

As indicated in the preface to this book, all procedures are for use with the Student Version of SPSS 13.0 for Windows. Students who are using other versions of SPSS may need to make adjustments.

Defining, Entering, and Saving Numeric Data

As its name implies, *numeric data* consist of scores. In SPSS, *string data* consist of letters that make up words, abbreviations, and codes. For instance, if a researcher enters the name of each participant, he or she is entering *string data*. In this chapter, only numeric data for scores at the *scale level of measurement* will be entered into SPSS. (See Chapter 1 to review this level of measurement; the *scale level* in SPSS includes the traditional *interval* and *ratio levels*.) To enter and save numeric data for a scale variable, follow these steps:

Step 1: Start SPSS by clicking on "Start" at the lower-left corner of the screen and then clicking on "SPSS for Windows."[1]

After executing Step 1, you should see the dialog box shown in Figure 2.1 on the next page. By default, SPSS assumes you will want to "Open an existing data source" (notice the cir-

---

[1] You may have to first click on "All Programs" to get a list of programs from which you can select "SPSS for Windows."

cle with a dot in it in Figure 2.1). Because you will be entering new data (instead of working with data that were previously saved), follow the next step.

Step 2: Click on the circle to the left of "Type in data" (see the arrow in Figure 2.1), and then click OK.

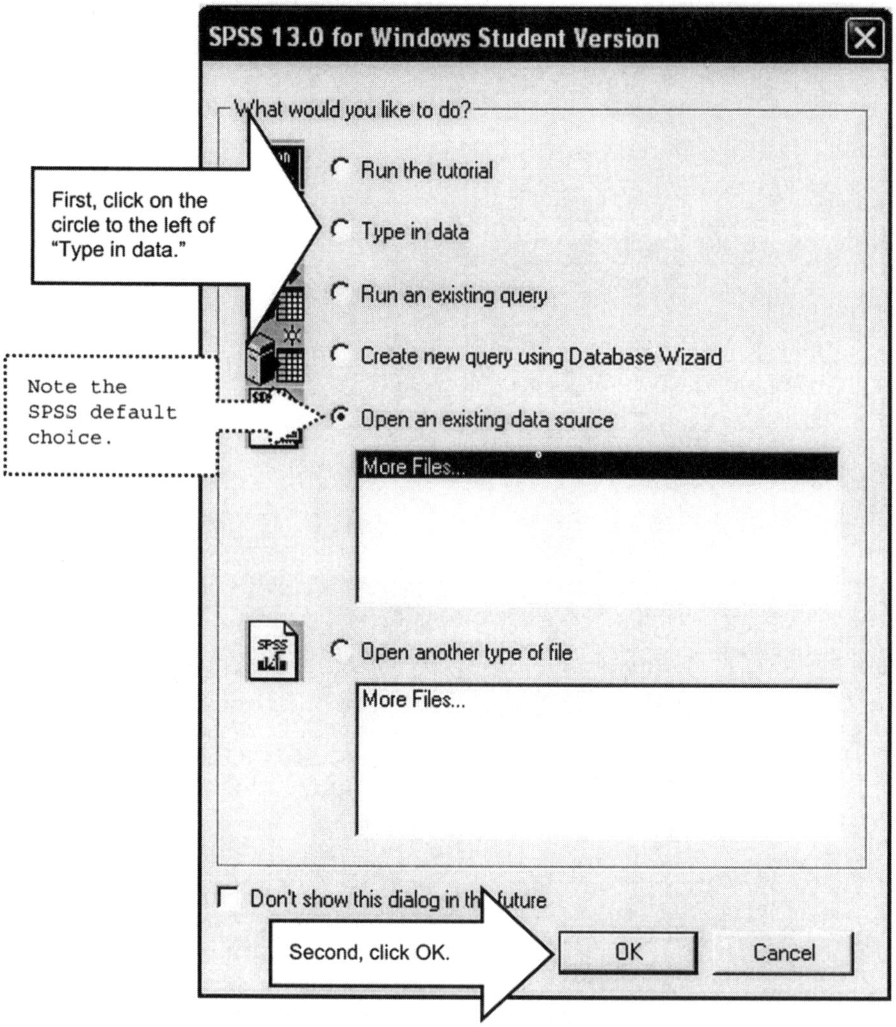

Figure 2.1. Sequence for Step 2.

After executing Step 2, the SPSS "Data Editor" shown in Figure 2.2 on the next page will appear.

Step 3: Click on the "Variable View" tab to be sure you are in the Variable View screen.

See the arrow in Figure 2.2 on the next page. Also, see Information Box 2.1 on the next page.

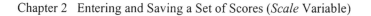

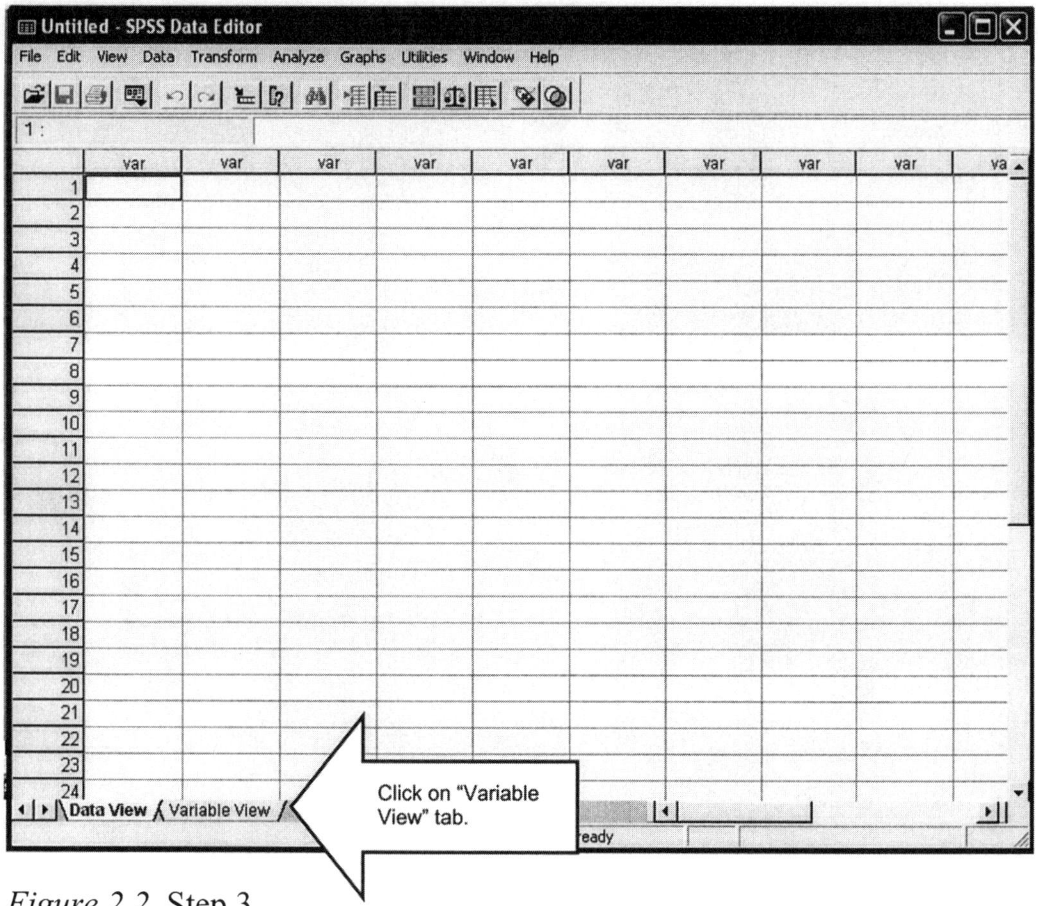

Figure 2.2. Step 3.

Information Box 2.1
The Functions of the Variable View and Data View Modes (Screens)

Figure 2.2 above shows the SPSS Data Editor. The Data Editor has two screens, which can be accessed by clicking on the tabs to the left of the arrow in Figure 2.2 above.

1. In the *Variable View* screen, you will name and label a variable, as indicated in Steps 4 and 5 on the next page. To be sure you are in it, click on the tab that says "Variable View."

2. In the *Data View* screen, you will be entering scores, as indicated in Steps 6 through 8. You can switch back and forth between the Variable View and Data View screens by clicking on the tabs at the lower-left corner of the Data Editor screen. You can try switching back and forth now, but be sure to click on "Variable View" again before proceeding with the remaining steps in this chapter.

Scores on an Attitude Toward School scale with possible scores ranging from 0 to 10 will be used in this chapter. To give this variable a brief name, follow Step 4.

Step 4: Name the variable by typing the word "School."

After executing Step 4 (giving the variable a brief name), the word "School" should be in the cell (i.e., rectangular box) at the upper-left corner. ***See the arrow for Step 4 in Figure 2.3 on the next page***. Then follow Step 5 to give the variable a longer name (i.e., label).

Step 5: Click on the empty cell just below the word "Label," and type the words "Attitude Toward School."[2]

After executing Step 5, you should see the words you typed in the cell under the word "Label." ***See the arrow for Step 5 in Figure 2.3 on the next page.***

Step 6: Click on the "Data View" tab at the lower-left corner of the Data Editor.

After executing Step 6, you will be in the Data View mode of the SPSS Data Editor (see Information Box 2.1 on the previous page for the difference between Variable View and Data View modes). ***See the arrow for Step 6 in Figure 2.3 on the next page***.

Information Box 2.2
SPSS Default for Levels of Measurement

> By default, SPSS assumes that you are entering data at the *scale* level of measurement (i.e., the traditional interval and ratio levels; see Chapter 1 for more information on levels of measurement). Because you will be entering data for a scale variable in this chapter, no special action on your part is necessary. In other words, you do not need to indicate that the data are at the scale level; SPSS already assumes that they are at this level.

---

[2] You can also move to the cell under the word "Label" by repeatedly pressing the Tab key or the right-arrow key on the keyboard.

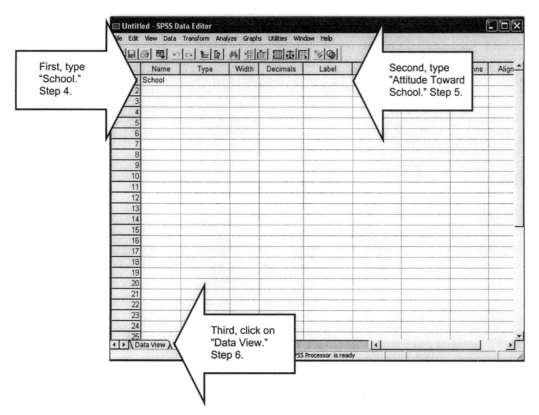

Figure 2.3. Steps 4, 5, and 6.

Figure 2.4 below shows the Data View screen, which will appear after you execute Step 6. The Data View screen is the screen that allows you to enter data (e.g., scores).

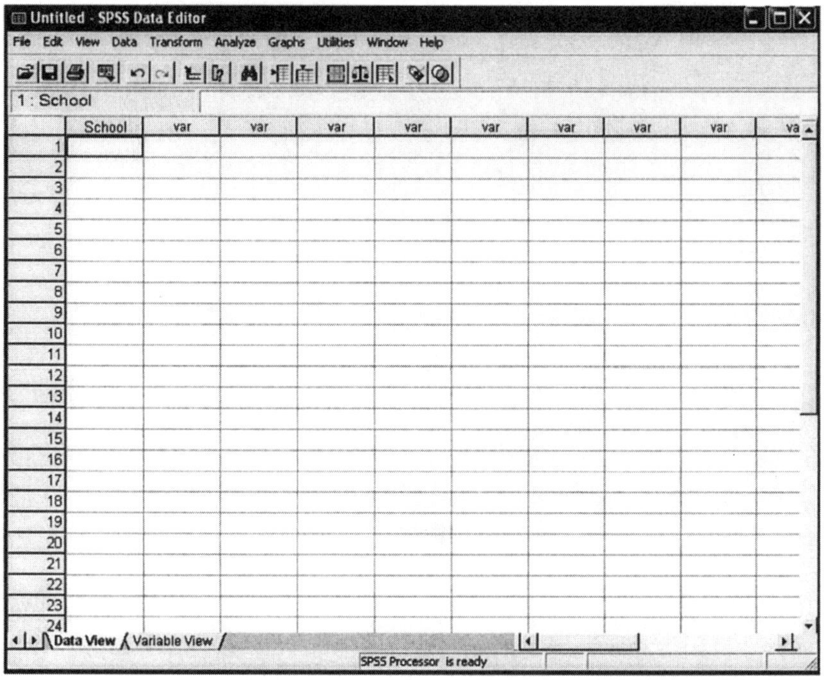

Figure 2.4. The Data View screen produced by executing Step 6.

Before proceeding to the next step, consider the Attitude Toward School scores in Table 2.1 below. The scores were obtained with a scale that contains ten positive statements regarding school (e.g., "I look forward to going to school in the morning."). For each statement, each of 20 students checked "yes" or "no." For each "yes," a student obtained a score of "1." Then, these scores were summed to get a total score for each student. Thus, a score of 6 indicates that the student checked "yes" for six of the ten positive statements about school. Obviously, the scores can range from zero to ten. Like scores on a multiple-choice test (see Chapter 1), these scores are assumed to be at the *interval* (i.e., *scale*) level of measurement.

Table 2.1
Attitude Toward School Scores for 20 Students on a Scale from 0 to 10

8	9	10	2	5	6	6	7	6	2
1	6	9	4	6	6	5	6	10	0

Step 7: Type the number "8" (the first score in Table 2.1 above), and then press the Tab key or Enter key on your keyboard.[3]

After executing Step 7, the number 8 should be in the upper-left cell, and the cell below it should be highlighted by having darker lines around it. ***See the arrow in Figure 2.5 below.***

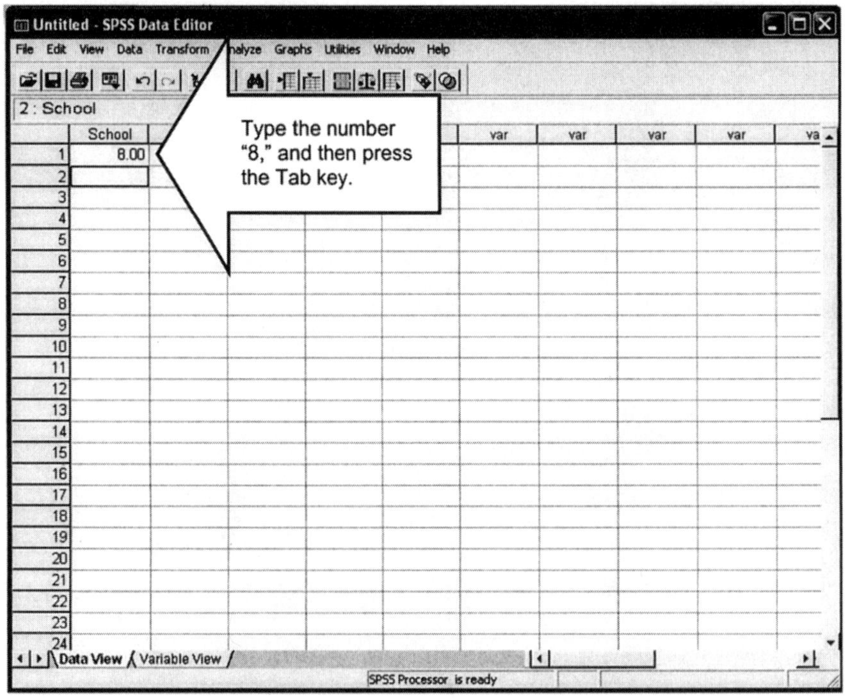

Figure 2.5. Step 7.

---

[3] Instead of pressing the Tab or Enter key after each data entry, you can also press the down-arrow key. You can also move from cell to cell to enter data using the mouse.

Step 8: Type the remaining scores (9, 10, 2, etc.) from Table 2.1 on the previous page, remembering to press the Tab or Enter key after typing each one.

See Figure 2.6 below.

After executing Steps 7 and 8, the Data Editor should look like this:

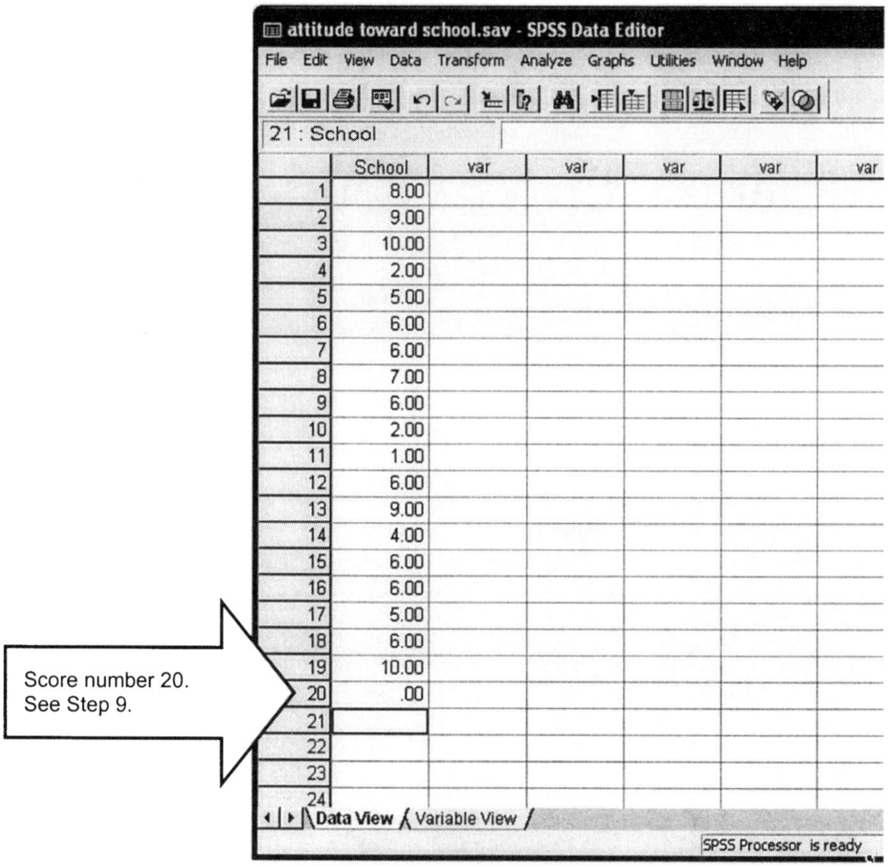

Figure 2.6. The Data View screen after all the scores are entered. See Steps 7, 8, and 9.

Step 9: Check the accuracy of your entries.

Execute this step by doing two things. First, check to make sure that you have entered 20 scores. Notice that the scores are numbered from 1 to 20 in the Data Editor in Figure 2.6 above. (Put another way, the numbers from 1 to 20 represent the 20 participants, each of whom has one score.) Then, compare each score you entered with the scores in Table 2.1 on the previous page.

The time to check the entries is now—not after you find that your answers are incorrect. A major source of errors when using SPSS is the failure to carefully check to see that all scores have been entered correctly.

Step 10: Name and save the data file you created.

To execute this step, click on the word "File" near the upper-left corner of the screen, and then click on "Save As."[4] Next, type the words "Attitude Toward School" and click "Save."

You may want to save to an external device such as a floppy disk or CD. Note that you will need this data file in subsequent chapters.

Step 11: Close SPSS by clicking on the red box with the X in the upper-right corner of the screen.

Exercise for Chapter 2

1. You will be entering the scores shown in Table 2.2 below (for attitude toward math) into SPSS.

Table 2.2
Attitude Toward Math Scores for 20 Students on a Scale from 0 to 10

2	10	6	0	6	4	3	4	5	1
1	5	7	1	1	3	4	4	6	1

Specifically, do the following:

   a. Start SPSS (see Step 1).

   b. Indicate that you want to "Type in data" (see Step 2).

   c. Click on the Variable View tab (see Step 3).

   d. Name the variable. Give it the name "Math" (see Step 4).

   e. Label the variable. Give it the label "Attitude Toward Math" (see Step 5).

   f. Switch to the Data View screen in the Data Editor (see Step 6).

   g. Type in the scores shown in Table 2.2 above. Enter the scores in order, starting with the scores in the first row: 2, 10, 6, and so on (see Steps 7 and 8).

   h. Check the accuracy of your entries (see Step 9).

   i. Save the data set, giving it the name "Attitude Toward Math" (see Step 10).

   j. If your instructor wants to check your work, he or she may ask you to print out the data you have entered. You can do this by clicking on the letter "p" while holding down the CTRL key and then clicking on OK (or by clicking on "File" near the upper-left corner of the screen, then clicking on "Print," and then clicking on OK).

   k. Close SPSS (see Step 11).

---

[4] Instead of clicking on "File," you can also first click on the icon near the top of the screen that looks like a floppy disk.

2. You will be entering the data set shown in Table 2.3 below (for height) into SPSS.

Table 2.3

Height in Inches (i.e., scores) for 20 Students on a Scale from 0 to 10

62	52	72	70	67	66	63	70	50	62
60	49	74	70	66	67	66	71	64	69

Specifically, do the following:

   a. Start SPSS (see Step 1).

   b. Indicate that you want to "Type in data" (see Step 2).

   c. Click on the Variable View tab (see Step 3).

   d. Name the variable. Give it the name "Height" (see Step 4).

   e. Label the variable. Give it the label "Height in Inches" (see Step 5).

   f. Switch to the Data View screen in the Data Editor (see Step 6).

   g. Type in the scores (i.e., inches) shown in Table 2.3 above. Enter them in order, starting with the scores in the first row: 62, 52, 72, and so on (see Steps 7 and 8).

   h. Check the accuracy of your entries (see Step 9).

   i. Save the data set, giving it the name "Height in Inches" (see Step 10).

   j. If your instructor wants to check your work, he or she may ask you to print out the data you have entered. You can do this by clicking on the letter "p" while holding down the CTRL key and then clicking on OK (or by clicking on "File" near the upper-left corner of the screen, then clicking on "Print," and then clicking on OK).

   k. Close SPSS (see Step 11).

Notes:

Chapter 3

Frequency Distribution

Learning objectives:

1. Open a saved data file.
2. Create a frequency distribution, including percentages and cumulative percentages.
3. Save the SPSS output.
4. Print out the SPSS output.
5. Format an SPSS frequency distribution output for presentation in a research report.

Introductory Comment

After completing Chapter 2, you should have three data files saved: one for "Attitude Toward School," one for "Attitude Toward Math," and one for "Height in Inches." The first two of these files will be used in this chapter.

Definition of "Frequency Distribution"

In this chapter, you will be creating a *frequency distribution*. A basic frequency distribution is a statistical table that lists the scores in one column and shows the number of participants who earned each score in the next column. In SPSS, a frequency distribution shows additional information relating to each score (such as the percentage of participants who earned each score).

Creating an SPSS Frequency Distribution

Step 1: Start SPSS by clicking on "Start" at the lower-left corner of the screen and then clicking on "SPSS for Windows."[1]

Notice that by default, SPSS assumes you want to "Open an existing data source." This is indicated by the circle to the left of "Open an existing data source" being filled in (see the circle just above the arrow in Figure 3.1 on the next page). In this chapter, you will be analyzing data in the files you saved when working through Chapter 2. Thus, you do not need to change the choice ("Open an existing data source") already selected by SPSS.

---

[1] You may have to first click on "All Programs" to get a list of programs from which you can select "SPSS for Windows."

Step 2: Locate the "Attitude Toward School" file that you saved in Chapter 2 and double-click on it.

See the arrow in Figure 3.1 below. Double-click on the file name. (If you do not see the Attitude Toward School data file listed, click OK to get a complete list of available data files. Then, double-click on the Attitude Toward School file. If you saved the data file to an external medium such as a floppy or CD when working through Chapter 2, see Information Box 3.1 below and Figure 3.2 on the next page for additional instructions.)

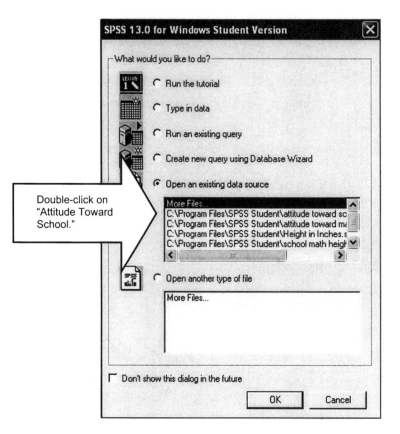

Figure 3.1. Step 2.

Information Box 3.1
Procedure If the Data Files Were Saved on an External Medium, Such As a Floppy Disk

If you saved the data files that you created when working through Chapter 2 to an external medium such as a floppy disk or CD, click OK in Step 2, which will open the "Open File" dialog box. Switch from "Look in SPSS (Student)" by clicking on the down arrow. Then, for a floppy, for instance, double-click on "3½ Floppy (A)" to get a list of the files you saved on it. Then, double-click on "Attitude Toward School" to open the file. *See the arrows in Figure 3.2 on the next page.*

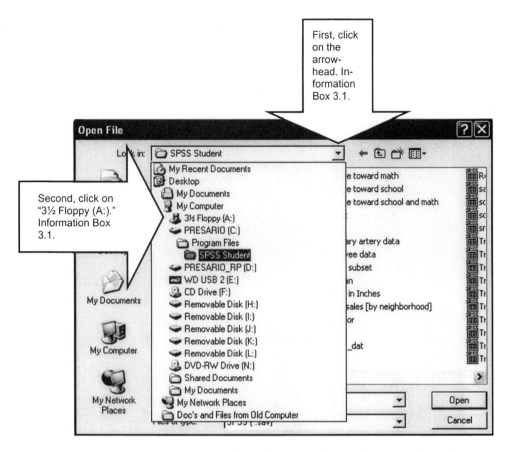

Figure 3.2. Locating a data file saved to a floppy disk after clicking on "File" and "Open." See Information Box 3.1.

After executing Step 2, you should see the data you previously saved, as shown in Figure 3.3. on the next page. (If the data are not on the screen, click on the "Data View" tab near the lower-left corner to switch from "Variable View" to "Data View.")

To create a frequency distribution for Attitude Toward School, follow the remaining steps.

Step 3: Click on "Analyze" near the top of the screen.

See the arrow in Figure 3.3 on the next page. After clicking on "Analyze," a drop-down menu will appear.

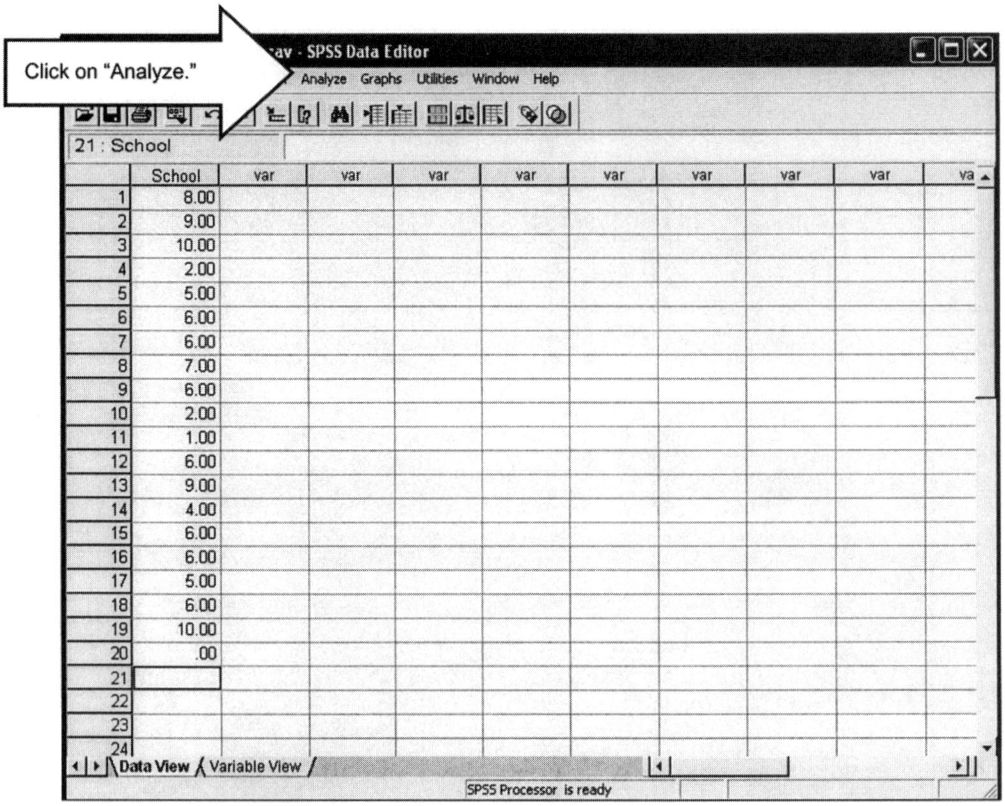

Figure 3.3. Step 3.

Step 4: From the drop-down menu that appears after you execute Step 3, use the mouse to put the cursor on the phrase "Descriptive Statistics." Then, click on "Frequencies...."

See the arrows in Figure 3.4 on the next page.

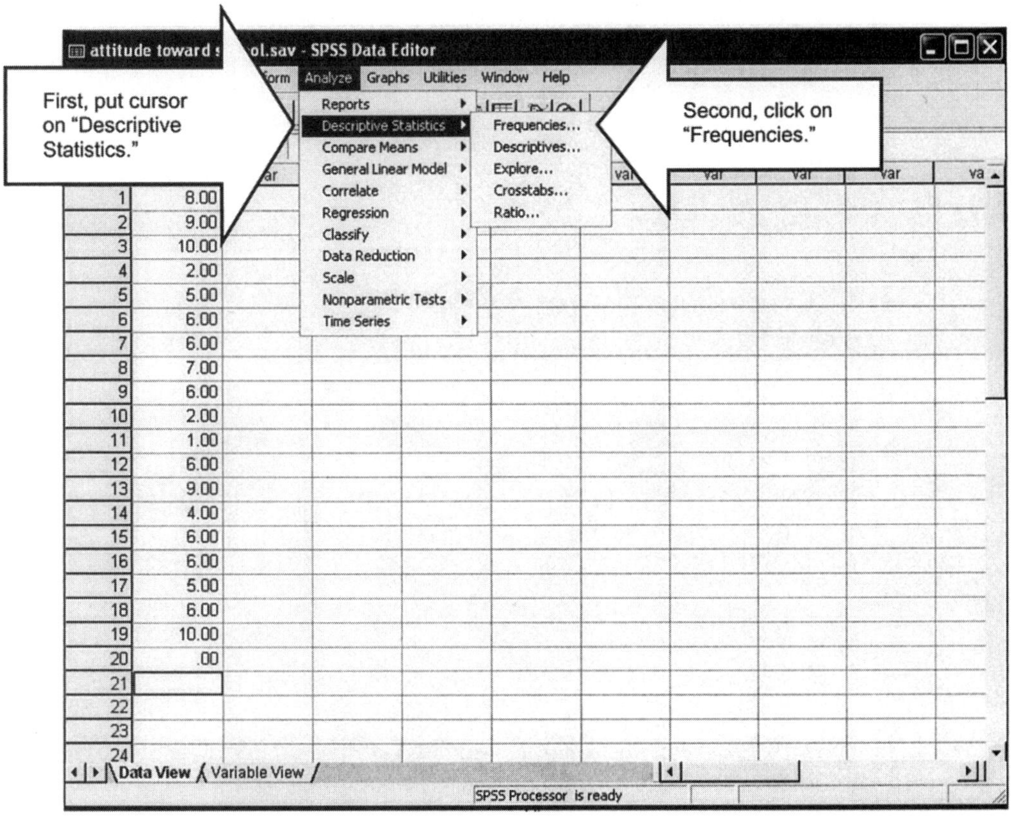

Figure 3.4. Step 4.

Executing Step 4 will produce the "Frequencies..." dialog box on the screen.

Step 5: Click on the arrowhead in the "Frequencies..." dialog box, which will appear after you execute Step 4.

Before clicking, notice that "Attitude Toward School" is in the box on the left. This box shows a list of the variables that have been saved in a given data file. At this point, there is only one variable in the data file you opened in Step 2, so you need only to click on the arrow to move the name of the variable from the left-hand box to the right-hand box. ***See the arrow in Figure 3.5 on the next page.***

Moving a variable from the left-hand box to the right-hand "Variable(s)" box selects the variable for which you want to a create frequency distribution. In the next chapter, you will see a list with more than one variable from which you will choose the variable to be analyzed.

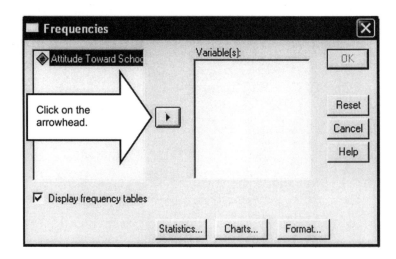

Figure 3.5. Step 5.

Step 6: Click OK.

See Figure 3.6 below.

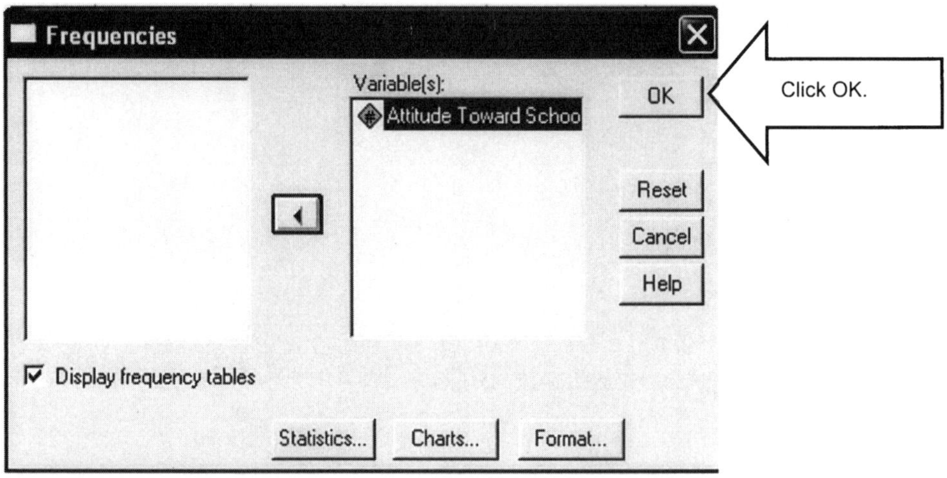

Figure 3.6. Step 6.

After executing Step 6, you should see the SPSS output, which is the frequency distribution shown in Figure 3.7 on the next page.

→ **Frequencies**

Statistics

Attitude Toward School

N	Valid	20
	Missing	0

Attitude Toward School

		Frequency	Percent	Valid Percent	Cumulative Percent
Valid	.00	1	5.0	5.0	5.0
	1.00	1	5.0	5.0	10.0
	2.00	2	10.0	10.0	20.0
	4.00	1	5.0	5.0	25.0
	5.00	2	10.0	10.0	35.0
	6.00	7	35.0	35.0	70.0
	7.00	1	5.0	5.0	75.0
	8.00	1	5.0	5.0	80.0
	9.00	2	10.0	10.0	90.0
	10.00	2	10.0	10.0	100.0
	Total	20	100.0	100.0	

> Because no one obtained a score of 3, SPSS has omitted it. You should include it when formatting. Compare with Table 3.1 on page 26.

Figure 3.7. Unformatted frequency distribution (SPSS output).

Step 7: Print the output.

The output can be printed in one of three ways: (a) by clicking on the letter "p" while holding down the CTRL key and then clicking on OK, *or* (b) by clicking on "File" near the upper-left corner of the screen, then clicking on "Print" and then clicking on OK, *or* (c) by clicking on the icon near the top of the screen that looks like a printer and then clicking on OK.

Step 8: Save the output.[2]

To execute Step 8:

a. Click on "File" near the upper-left corner of the screen.

b. Click on "Save As."[3]

c. Name the output "Attitude Toward School Frequency Distribution." *See the arrow in Figure 3.8 on the next page.*

d. Click on "Save." *See the arrow in Figure 3.8 on the next page.*

---

[2] If you need to reopen the output that you are saving, (a) click on "File," (b) click on "Open," and (c) click on "Output." Double-click on the name of the output, which is "Attitude Toward School Frequency Distribution" in this example.

[3] If you will be saving to an external medium such as a floppy disk or CD, click on the arrow to the right of "Save in" near the top of the screen, and select the appropriate medium such as drive A for a floppy disk.

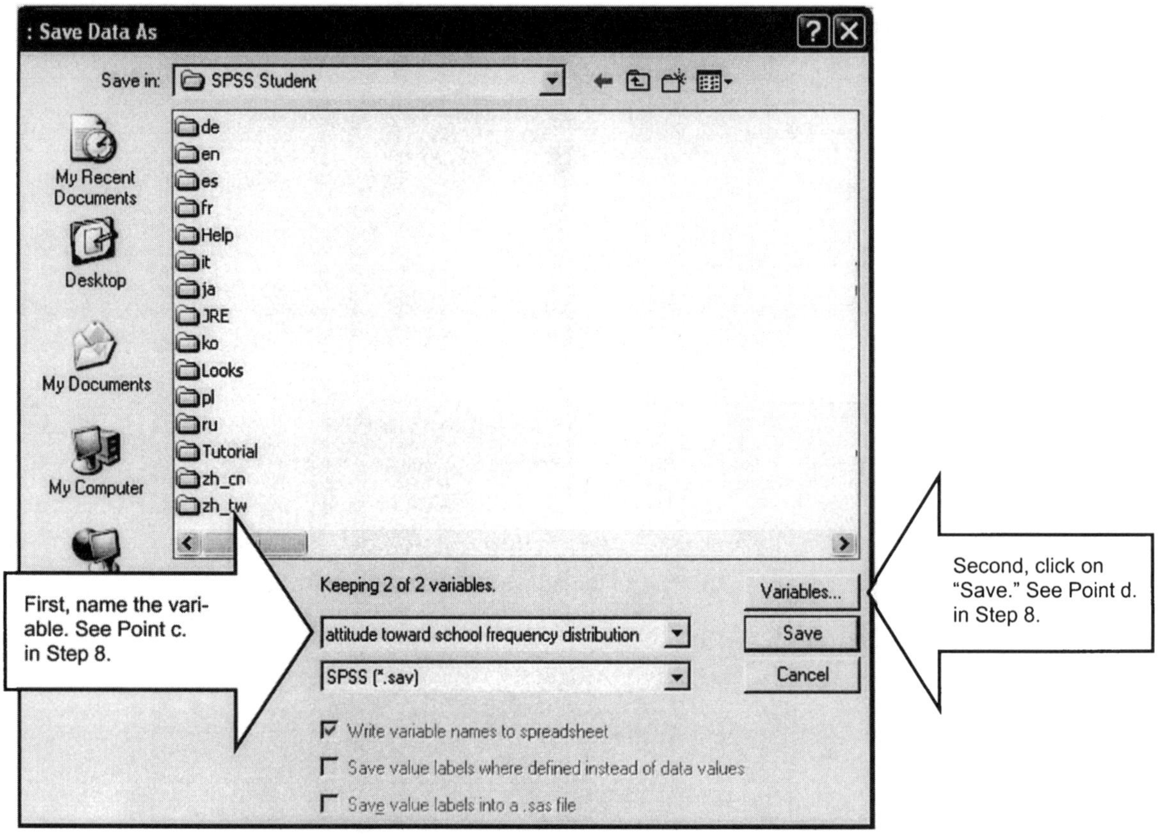

Figure 3.8. Points c. and d. in Step 8. Execute after clicking on "File" and "Save As."

Interpreting the SPSS Output

Notice the following features of the output in Figure 3.7 on the previous page.

1. In SPSS, the symbol "N" stands for "number of cases" (i.e., the number of participants; see the small box near the top of the output in Figure 3.7 on the previous page). In contrast with SPSS, the traditional symbols used by statisticians are:[4]

a. An uppercase italicized N for the number of cases in a population (e.g., if the population of a class of students consists of 20 students and all 20 were studied, then $N = 20$).

b. A lowercase italicized n for the number of cases in a sample (e.g., if the population consists of 40 sixth-grade students in a school but only a sample of 20 were studied, then $n = 20$).[5]

---

[4] As you will learn later in this chapter and throughout most of the rest of this book, SPSS provides *raw, unformatted* output, which you should format to be consistent with standard statistical reporting.

[5] When a letter is italicized, it is a statistical symbol; when it is not italicized, it is only a letter of the alphabet.

2. In the output in the large box in Figure 3.7 on page 23, note the following.

   a. The first column shows the scores from .00 to 10.00.

   b. The second column shows the frequency (i.e., number of participants) that earned each score (e.g., 2 participants earned a score of 5).

   c. The third column shows the percent that earned each score (e.g., 10% earned a score of 5).

   d. Ignore the fourth column: Valid Percent. (All cases in all exercises in this book will be valid.)

   e. The last column shows the cumulative percents, whose symbol is *cum%*. For instance, for a score of 5, the cumulative percent is 35%. This means that a participant with a score of 5 scored as high as or higher than 35% of the participants in the study.[6] In layperson terms, it is sufficient to say that a participant with a score of 5 scored higher than 35% of the other participants.

Formatting an SPSS Frequency Distribution for a Research Report

SPSS provides raw output that is usually *not* formatted in a conventional style for presentation in a research report. Table 3.1 on the next page shows conventional formatting consistent with APA style (see Information Box 3.2). The most efficient way to create a formatted frequency distribution is to use the "Table" function in a word-processing program such as Word.® SPSS cannot be used to do formatting.

Information Box 3.2
Consistency with the Publication Manual of the American Psychological Association

The most popular style manual for formatting statistical output for publication in research reports in the social and behavioral sciences is the *Publication Manual of the American Psychological Association* (APA). The formatting suggestions in this book are consistent with the guidelines in the APA manual. Copies of the manual are available for purchase at most college bookstores. Visit www.apa.org to purchase a copy online.

---

[6] In standardized testing, this is called a "percentile rank" (i.e., a *cum%* of 35 is equivalent to a percentile rank of 35).

Table 3.1

Formatted Frequency Distribution of Attitude Toward School Scores for the Output in Figure 3.7 on Page 23

Score (X)	f	%	Cum%
10	2	10.0	100.0
9	2	10.0	90.0
8	1	5.0	80.0
7	1	5.0	75.0
6	7	35.0	70.0
5	2		35.0
4	1		25.0
3	0		20.0
2	2		20.0
1	1		10.0
0	1	5.0	5.0
	N = 20	100.0	

Include the score of "3" with a frequency of zero even though it is omitted in the SPSS output in Figure 3.7 on page 23.

In formatting the raw SPSS output in order to create Table 3.1 above, the following was done:

1. The scores in the first column were rearranged, putting the highest score at the top.
2. All scores from the highest to the lowest earned are shown, including a score of "3," which has a frequency of zero and was omitted in the SPSS output. ***See the arrows in Figure 3.7 on page 23 and in Table 3.1 above.***
3. The first column was labeled with the word "Score" and the italicized uppercase letter "X," which is the statistical symbol for "score."
4. The second column was labeled with the italicized lowercase letter "f," which is the statistical symbol for "frequency."
5. The third and fourth columns were labeled with the symbols "%" and "Cum%."
6. The table was given a number (i.e., Table 3.1) placed above the table.
7. A caption (i.e., a descriptive title such as "*Formatted Frequency Distribution of....*") was placed on the lines below the table number. The caption is in italics with the first letter of important words capped. The title does *not* end with a period.

Exercise for Chapter 3

1. You will be preparing a frequency distribution for Attitude Toward Math scores that you saved in the first question in the Exercise for Chapter 2.

   Specifically, do the following:

   a. Start SPSS (see Step 1).

   b. Locate the "Attitude Toward Math" data file that you saved in Chapter 2 of this book and open it (see Step 2).

   c. Click on "Analyze" near the top of the screen (see Step 3).

   d. Put the cursor on "Descriptive Statistics." Then, click on "Frequencies…" (see Step 4).

   e. Click on the arrowhead in the "Frequencies" screen (see Step 5).

   f. Click OK (see Step 6).

   g. Print the output (see Step 7).

   h. Save the output, giving it the name "Attitude Toward Math Frequency Distribution" (see Step 8). Format the SPSS output to be consistent with the formatting in Table 3.1 on the previous page. Note that scores of 8 and 9 were not obtained by any of the participants. To be consistent with traditional reporting, include these scores in your formatted frequency distribution and show that they each have a frequency of zero. To format the distribution, use a word processing program or use lined paper and a pencil.

Notes:

Chapter 4

Histogram

Learning objectives:
1. Add data for a second variable to a saved data file.
2. Create a histogram using SPSS.
3. Distinguish between the terms *histogram* and *bar graph.*
4. Examine the shape of a distribution displayed in a histogram.
5. Superimpose a normal curve on a histogram.
6. Format an SPSS histogram output for presentation in a research report.
7. Distinguish between the terms *graph* and *figure.*

Introductory Comment

Up to this point in this book, you have created data files, each of which has data for only one variable for one group of participants. In practice, researchers typically collect data on several variables for one or more groups of participants. In this chapter, you will learn how to add data for a second variable to a data file you previously saved with only one variable. Then, you will learn how to select one of the two variables for analysis in order to create a histogram.

Definition of "Histogram"

A *histogram* is a statistical figure (i.e., a drawing depicting statistics) that consists of vertical bars. When analyzing frequencies (i.e., counts of how many participants have each score), the heights of the bars are proportionate to the frequencies. See Figure 4.6 on page 34 for an example of a histogram.

Creating an SPSS Histogram

Step 1: Start SPSS by clicking on "Start" at the lower-left corner of the screen and then clicking on "SPSS for Windows."[1]

Step 2: Locate the "Attitude Toward School" file that you saved in Chapter 2, and double-click on it to open it.

---

[1] You may have to click on "All Programs" after clicking on "Start" to get a list of programs from which you can select "SPSS for Windows."

To review how to take this step, see the directions for Step 2 in Chapter 3. If you are unable to locate the file, you will need to recreate it by executing the steps in Chapter 2.

Step 3: Click on "Variable View" to make sure you are in the Variable View mode.

See the arrow for Step 3 in Figure 4.1 below.

Step 4: Then click on the cell just below the word "School" and name the second variable "Absences."

See the arrow for Step 4 in Figure 4.1 below. Note that you will be adding data for a second variable named "Absences."[2] Notice the number "2" to the left of the word "Absences" in Figure 4.1. This identifies the variable as Variable Number 2 in SPSS.

Step 5: Click on the cell below "Attitude Toward School" and label the second variable "Days Absent from School."

See the arrow for Step 5 in Figure 4.1 below.

Step 6: Click on the "Data View" tab near the lower-left corner of the Data Editor.

See the arrow for Step 6 in Figure 4.1 below.

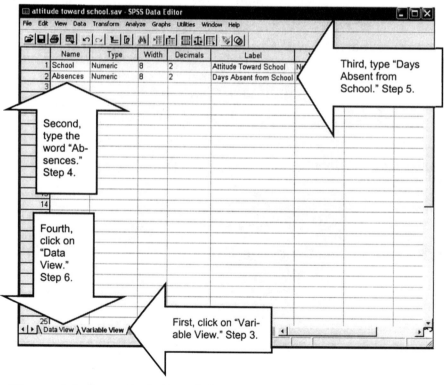

Figure 4.1. Steps 3, 4, 5, and 6.

---

[2] Note that "Days Absent from School" is a *scale* variable in SPSS. See Chapter 1 to review this concept.

After executing Step 6, your screen should look like the one in Figure 4.2 below.

Step 7: Enter the scores from Table 4.1 immediately below into SPSS.

In the first blank cell below the word "Absences," type in the first score (a score of 4) from Table 4.1 below. Then press Enter (or press the down arrow on the keyboard), type in the next score (a score of 3), and so on. *See the arrow in Figure 4.2 below.*

Table 4.1

Days Absent from School for 20 Students

4	3	3	12	13	6	7	9	8	11
8	4	0	5	7	6	5	6	2	9

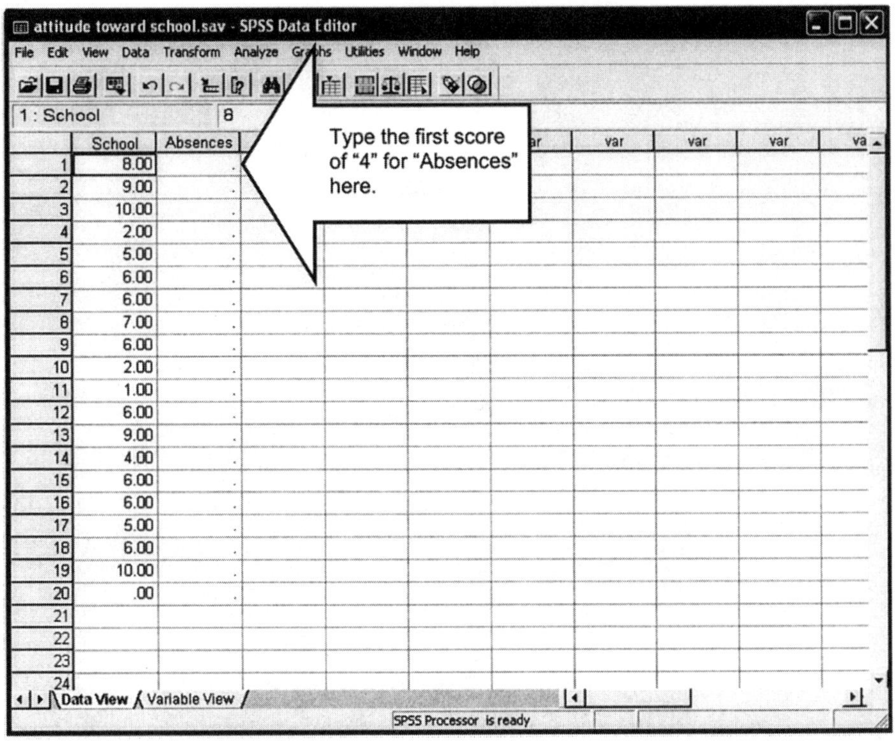

Figure 4.2. Step 7.

After executing Step 7, your screen should look like the one in Figure 4.3 below.

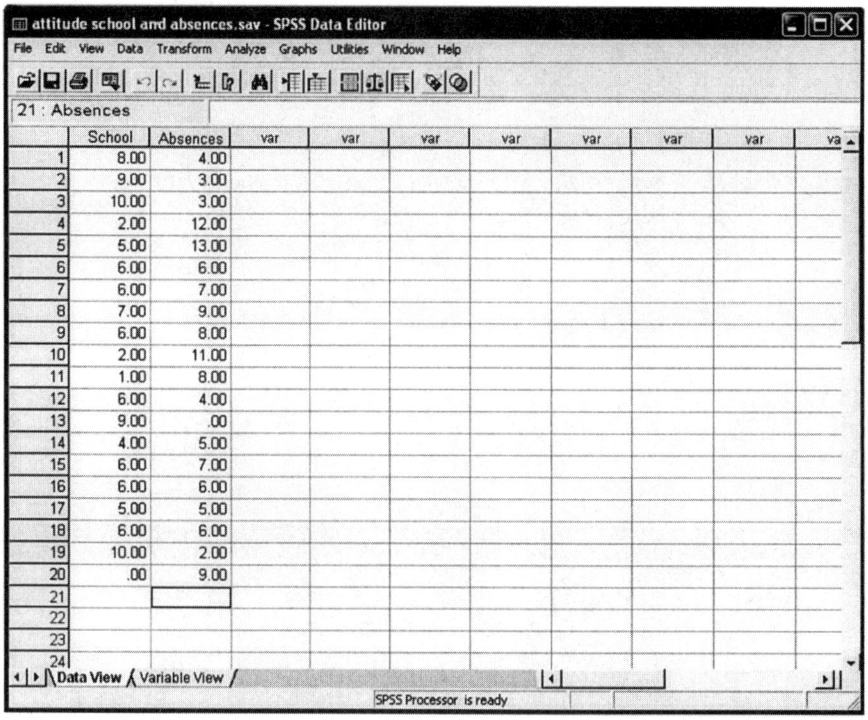

Figure 4.3. Two sets of scores. The set for "Absences" was added in Step 7.

Step 8: Save the modified data file with a new name.

Click on "File." Then, click on "Save As...," and name it "Attitude School and Absences." Note that the file has been modified by adding an additional variable (absences), so the file should have a new name to indicate this. Thus, the new file name includes the word "Absences." Finally, click on "Save."

Step 9: Click on "Graphs."

See the arrow for Step 9 in Figure 4.4 on the next page.

After executing Step 9, a drop-down menu will appear on the screen.

Step 10: Click on "Histogram..." in the drop-down menu.

See the arrow for Step 10 in Figure 4.4 on the next page.

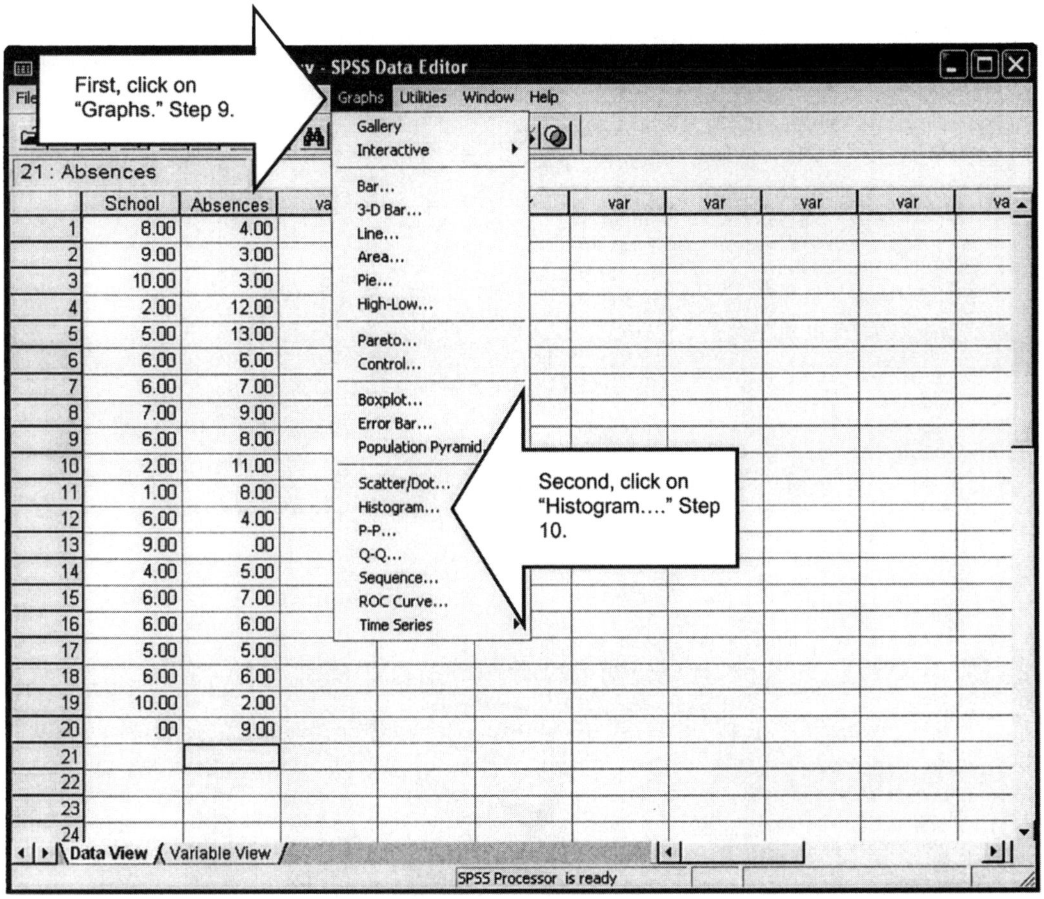

Figure 4.4. Steps 9 and 10.

Step 11: Move "Days Absent from School" from the list on the left to the "Variable" box on the right.

To execute Step 11, first click once on "Days Absent from School." (Doing this selects and highlights the name of the variable to be moved.) Then, click on the top arrowhead.[3] This will move the variable name "Days Absent from School" from the list of two variables on the left to the box labeled "Variable."[4] ***See the arrows in Figure 4.5 on the next page.***

Note that the variables moved to the "Variable" box are the variables that will be analyzed. By executing Step 11, you are telling SPSS that you want to analyze the variable named "Days Absent from School."

---

[3] You can also move a variable from the left to the right (when the arrowhead is pointing to the right) by double-clicking on the name of the variable.

[4] If you move the wrong variable from the left to the right, you can move it back to the left by reversing the procedure. Specifically, once you have moved a variable name to the right, the arrowhead in the small box will change directions to point left, allowing you to move the variable back to the left. You can practice moving variables from left to right at this point. However, be sure to end with "Days Absent from School" on the right before proceeding to the next step.

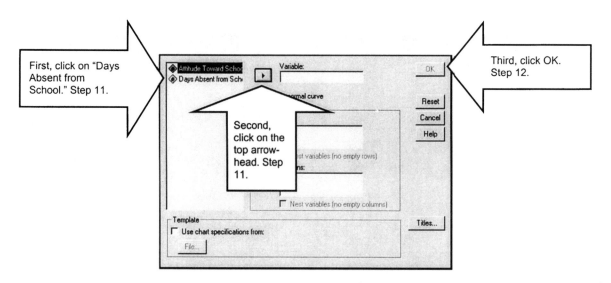

First, click on "Days Absent from School." Step 11.

Second, click on the top arrow-head. Step 11.

Third, click OK. Step 12.

Figure 4.5. Sequence for Steps 11 and 12.

Step 12: Click OK near the upper-right corner of the dialog box.

After executing Step 12, the SPSS output (a histogram) will appear. ***See Figure 4.6 below.***

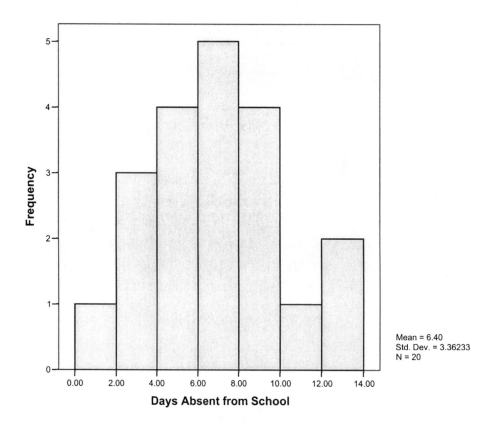

Figure 4.6. Histogram for frequency of days absent from school for 20 students.

Note that SPSS has automatically put the scores in groups. For instance, the first bar on the left is for this group of scores: 0 and 1; the next bar is for this group of scores: 2 and 3; and so on. Grouping scores keeps the histogram from getting too large from left to right (especially when scores have a wide range such as from 0 to 100).

Also, note that SPSS automatically calculates and reports the means and standard deviations associated with histograms (see the values to the right of the histogram in Figure 4.6 on the previous page). These are important statistics that can be calculated in several ways using SPSS, as will be illustrated and discussed in later chapters.

Step 13: Save the output.

To execute this step, click on the word "File" near the upper-left corner of the screen, and then click on "Save As...." Then, type this file name: "Days Absent Histogram." Then, click "Save." You may want to save to an external device such as a floppy disk or CD.

Information Box 4.1

Distinguishing Between a Histogram and a Bar Graph

While a histogram consists of vertical bars, it is important to note that a "histogram" is *not* a "bar graph." Notice that on the drop-down list in Figure 4.4 on page 33 there is a choice called "Bar...," which produces a bar graph—not a histogram. Here is a summary of points to remember:

1. A *histogram* consists of a set of vertical bars that touch each other. Histograms should be created for *scale variables* (see Chapter 1 to review the meaning of scale variables; days absent from school is a scale variable). Therefore, in Step 10, you selected "Histogram..." *not* "Bar...," which is also one of the choices in Figure 4.4.
2. A *bar graph* consists of vertical bars that do not touch. Bar graphs should be created for *categorical variables* (see Chapter 1 to review the meaning of categorical variables). Because Days Absent from School is *not* a categorical variable, it would be inappropriate to create a bar graph for this variable.

Interpreting the SPSS Output

Examining a Histogram for the Typical Score(s) and Range

Examining a histogram provides an overview of the distribution of scores (e.g., days absent from school). In the histogram in Figure 4.6 on the previous page, notice the middle of the distribution (i.e., the typical number of days absent, which have the tallest bars) as well as the range of absences from low to high.

Comparing a Histogram with the Normal Curve

One of the most important characteristics of a histogram is whether it approximates the *normal curve* (i.e., the familiar bell-shaped curve). This is one of the most important concepts in statistics because many of the statistical procedures you learn about in your statistics textbooks are based on this curve.

SPSS facilitates determining whether the distribution in a histogram approaches normality by allowing you to superimpose a normal curve on a histogram. *To see the normal curve imposed on a histogram, follow Steps 14 through 17 below.*

Step 14: If you have not already done so, close the output that shows the histogram you created earlier in this chapter.

To execute this step, click on the arrow in the red box near the upper right of the output screen. This will return you to the Data View screen.

Step 15: Click again on "Graphs," and then click on "Histogram...."

To review this process, see Steps 9 and 10 earlier in this chapter.

Step 16: Select "Days Absent from School" for analysis.

See Steps 11 and 12 in this chapter to review this process.

Step 17: Click on the small box to the left of "Display normal curve," and then click OK.

After you click on the box, a check mark will appear in it. *See the arrows in Figure 4.7 on the next page.*

After clicking OK, you will see the histogram shown in Figure 4.8 on the next page with the normal curve superimposed. As you can see in Figure 4.8 on the next page, the distribution in the histogram approximates the normal distribution.

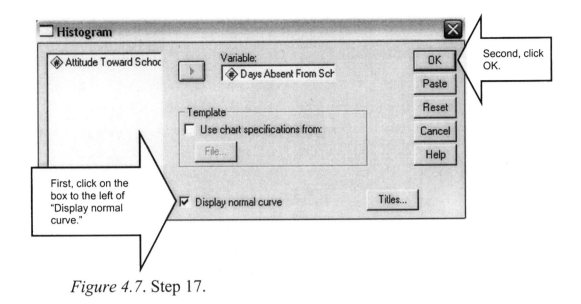

Figure 4.7. Step 17.

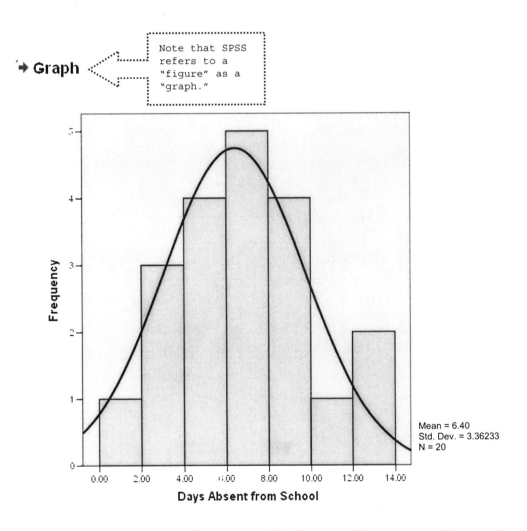

Figure 4.8. The histogram with the normal curve superimposed on it.

Formatting an SPSS Histogram for a Research Report

Terminology: "Graph" versus "Figure" for Labeling a Histogram

First, notice that SPSS refers to a histogram as a "graph." ***See the arrow in Figure 4.8 on the previous page.*** While the term "graph" is commonly used in the mass media and some fields such as business and economics, in the social and behavioral sciences, statistical drawings are referred to as "statistical figures" or simply as "figures."[5]

Giving a Histogram a Number and Caption (per APA)

All figures should be given a number and a descriptive title (known as a "caption"). As you can see, this is done in Figure 4.8 on the previous page.

Pay special attention to the following three items if you are following the style suggested in the *Publication Manual of the American Psychological Association.*[6]

1. The word "Figure," the figure number, and the caption are placed *below* the figure.[7]

2. The word "Figure" and the number are italicized and are followed by a period.

3. The title (caption) is *not* italicized and ends with a period.

Exercise for Chapter 4

1. You will be entering the scores shown in Table 4.2 (Grades in Algebra) below into SPSS and then creating a histogram.

Table 4.2

Grades in Algebra on a Scale from 0 (F) to 13 (A+) for 20 Students

1	3	10	1	3	3	13	10	9	2
2	3	7	12	0	3	6	4	5	4

---

[5] SPSS publications also use the term "chart," which is also referred to as a "figure" in the social and behavioral sciences.

[6] You can have SPSS title a figure by clicking on "Titles" near the lower-right corner of the dialog box in Figure 4.5 on page 34 before clicking on OK (Step 9). After clicking on "Titles," you can type in a title of your choice. However, it will *not* be properly formatted per APA style (e.g., the title will be above the figure and it will be called a "graph"). This is because SPSS uses its own style, not the style described in the *Publication Manual of the American Psychological Association.*

[7] In contrast, table numbers and captions are placed *above* tables in APA style.

Specifically, do the following:

 a. Start SPSS (see Step 1 in this chapter).

 b. Locate the "Attitude Toward Math" data file that you saved in Chapter 2 of this book and open the file (see Step 2). You will be adding the scores for algebra grades from Table 4.2 to this data file.

 c. Make sure you are in the Variable View mode (see Step 3).

 d. Name the new variable. Give it the name "Algebra" (see Step 4).

 e. Label the variable. Give it the label "Algebra Grades" (see Step 5).

 f. Switch to the Data View screen in the Data Editor (see Step 6).

 g. Type in the grades shown in Table 4.2 on page 38. Enter the grades in order, starting with the grades in the first row: 1, 3, 10, and so on (see Step 7).

 h. Save the modified data file (now with two variables), giving the data file the name "Attitude Toward Math and Algebra Grades" (see Step 8).

 i. Click on "Graphs" (see Step 9).

 j. On the drop-down menu, click on "Histogram…" (see Step 10).

 k. Move the variable "Algebra Grades" from the left-hand box to the right-hand box (see Step 11).

 l. Click OK (see Step 12).

 m. Print the output if your instructor will be collecting homework.

 n. Save the histogram (output), giving it the name "Algebra Grades Histogram" (Step 13).

 o. If your instructor wants you to use American Psychological Association style, format the histogram as described in this chapter under the heading "Formatting an SPSS Histogram for a Research Report."

 p. Examine the shape of the histogram with the normal curve superimposed on it (see Steps 14–17). Print out the output. On the printed copy, indicate whether you think the histogram has the shape of the normal curve.

Notes:

Chapter 5

Frequency Polygon

Learning objectives:
1. Create a frequency polygon using SPSS.
2. Distinguish between the terms "statistical figure" and "statistical table."
3. Format an SPSS frequency polygon for presentation in a research report.
4. Note potential for confusion in SPSS output when there is a score with a frequency of zero.
5. Create a polygon showing percentages instead of frequencies.

Definition of "Frequency Polygon"

A *frequency polygon* is a line drawing that shows the frequency (i.e., number of cases) for each score in a distribution. It shows the same information as a histogram (see Chapter 4) but does so with lines instead of bars.

Note that frequency distributions should be created only for *scale* variables.

Creating an SPSS Frequency Polygon

Step 1: Start SPSS by clicking on "Start" at the lower-left corner of the screen and then clicking on "SPSS for Windows."[1]

Step 2: Create a new data file for the scores shown in Table 5.1 below.

Chapter 2 shows how to create and save a new data file. When you create it, name the variable "Social" and label it "Social Anxiety."

Table 5.1
Social Anxiety Scores on a Scale from 10 to 20 for 20 Clients

10	19	20	13	13	14	15	14	17	16
18	11	12	16	15	14	17	16	20	18

---

[1] You may have to click on "Start" and then on "All Programs" to get a list of programs from which you can select "SPSS for Windows."

Step 3: Click on "Graphs."

See the arrow for Step 3 in Figure 5.1 below.

Step 4: Click on "Line..." from the drop-down menu.

See the arrow for Step 4 in Figure 5.1 below.

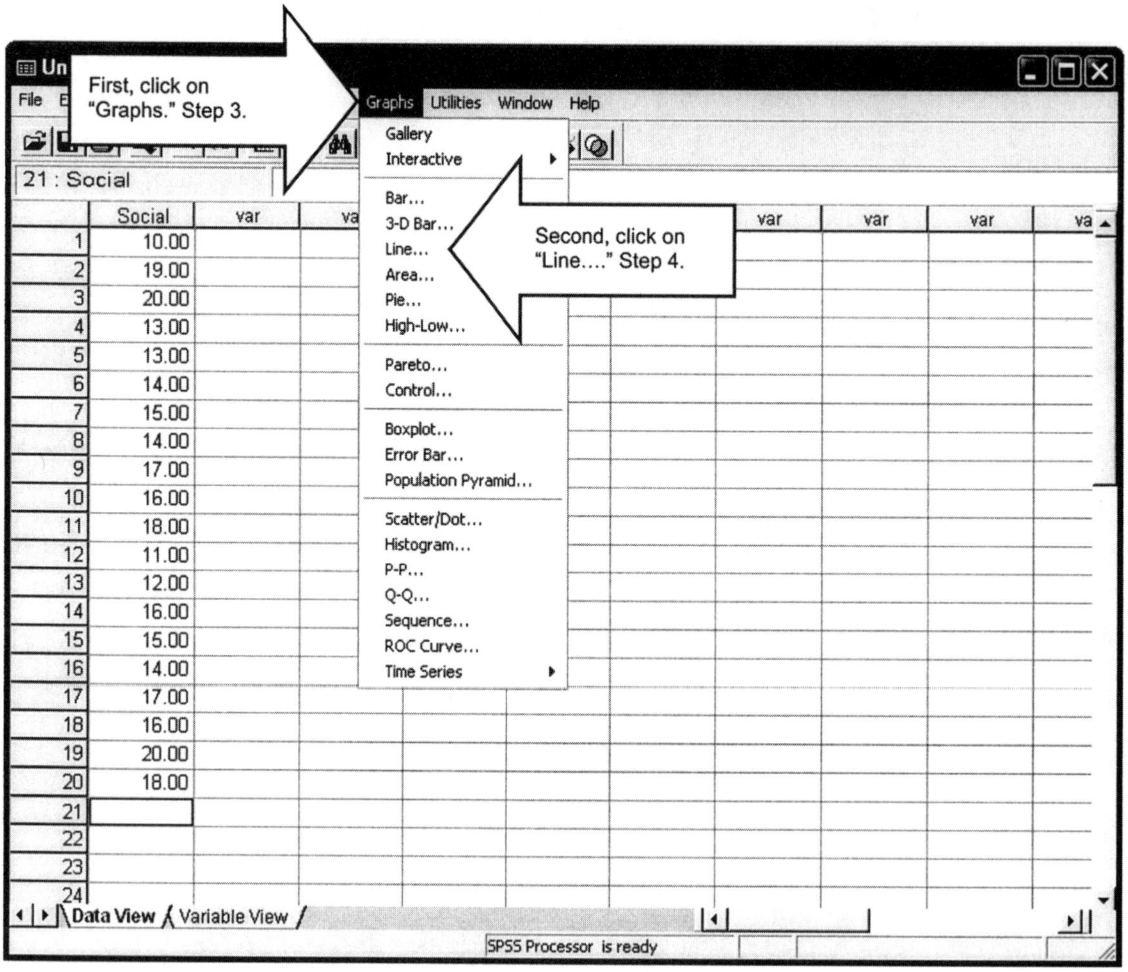

	Social	var	va			var	var	var	va
1	10.00								
2	19.00								
3	20.00								
4	13.00								
5	13.00								
6	14.00								
7	15.00								
8	14.00								
9	17.00								
10	16.00								
11	18.00								
12	11.00								
13	12.00								
14	16.00								
15	15.00								
16	14.00								
17	17.00								
18	16.00								
19	20.00								
20	18.00								
21									
22									
23									
24									

Menu: First, click on "Graphs." Step 3.
Graphs Utilities Window Help
Gallery
Interactive
Bar...
3-D Bar...
Line...   Second, click on "Line...." Step 4.
Area...
Pie...
High-Low...
Pareto...
Control...
Boxplot...
Error Bar...
Population Pyramid...
Scatter/Dot...
Histogram...
P-P...
Q-Q...
Sequence...
ROC Curve...
Time Series
Data View / Variable View
SPSS Processor is ready

Figure 5.1. Steps 3 and 4.

After executing Step 4, the "Line Charts" dialog box shown in Figure 5.2 on the next page will appear on the screen.

Step 5: Click on "Define."

See the arrow in Figure 5.2 on the next page. Note that by default, SPSS has selected the "Simple" line chart, which is the choice needed for creating a polygon for one set of scores. Clicking on "Define" confirms this choice.

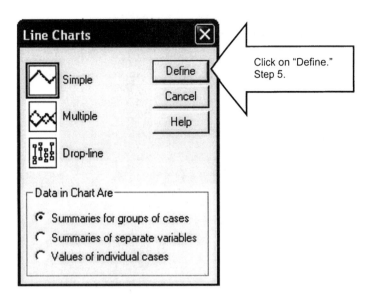

Figure 5.2. Step 5.

Step 6: Click on the arrowhead for "Category Axis."

See the arrow for Step 6 in Figure 5.3 below. This step will move the variable "Social Anxiety Scores" to the "Category Axis" dialog box. By executing Step 6, you are indicating that you want "Social Anxiety" to be on the horizontal axis in the frequency polygon.

Step 7: Click on OK.

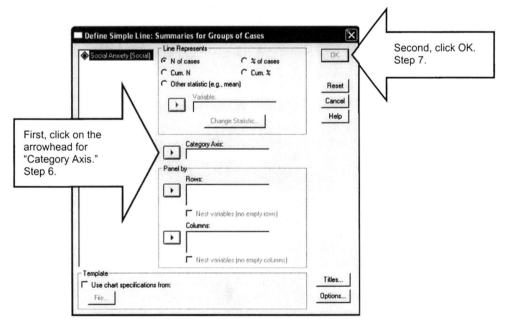

Figure 5.3. Steps 6 and 7.

After executing Step 7, an unformatted SPSS frequency polygon will appear on your screen. ***See the output in Figure 5.4 below.***

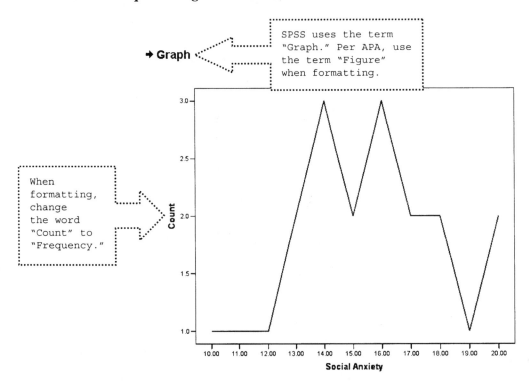

Figure 5.4. Unformatted SPSS frequency polygon.

Interpreting the SPSS Output

Like a histogram (see Chapter 4), a frequency polygon provides an overview of the distribution of scores (e.g., social anxiety scores). In the frequency polygon in Figure 5.4 above, notice the middle of the distribution as well as the range of social anxiety scores from low to high.

Formatting an SPSS Frequency Polygon for a Research Report

Terminology: "Graphs" versus "Figures" for Labeling a Polygon

Notice that SPSS refers to a polygon as a "graph." (***See the top arrow in Figure 5.4 above.***) While the term "graph" is commonly used in the mass media and some fields such as business and economics, in the social and behavioral sciences, statistical drawings are called "statistical figures" or simply "figures."[2]

---

[2] SPSS publications also use the term "chart," which is also referred to as a figure in the social and behavioral sciences.

Terminology: "Count" versus "Frequency"

Notice that SPSS labeled the vertical axis in Figure 5.4 on the previous page with the word "Count." While this is acceptable, it is conventional to use the term "Frequency" instead of "Count" in the social and behavioral sciences. ***See Figure 5.4 on the previous page***, where SPSS uses the term "Count," which should be changed to the word "Frequency." Note the statistical symbol for frequency is an italicized, lowercase letter f. You may substitute f for "frequency" when formatting.

Giving a Frequency Polygon a Number and Caption (per APA)

All figures should be given a number and a descriptive title (i.e., a "caption") such as this:

Figure 5.4. Unformatted SPSS frequency polygon.

Pay special attention to the following three items if you are following the style suggested in the *Publication Manual of the American Psychological Association*.

1. The word "Figure," the number, and caption are placed *below* the figure.
2. The word "Figure" and the number are italicized and are followed by a period.
3. The caption (i.e., title of the figure) is *not* italicized and ends with a period.

Information Box 5.1

Distinguishing Between a Statistical Figure and a Statistical Table

A *statistical figure*, such as a frequency polygon, is a drawing that represents statistical output. In contrast, a *statistical table* is an ordered set of statistical values without drawings.

Formatting a statistical table is different from formatting a statistical figure. Table 5.1 on page 41 is an example of a statistical table formatted per APA style. Notice that the table number and caption (i.e., title) are placed *above* a table, while a figure number and caption are placed *below* it.

Information Box 5.2

Creating a Polygon That Shows Percentages Instead of Frequencies

To create a polygon that shows percentages instead of frequencies, before executing Step 7 (before clicking OK), click on the circle to the left of "% of cases" (***see Figure 5.5 on the next page***). Then, click OK. A polygon showing percentages will be obtained (***see Figure 5.6 on the next page***).

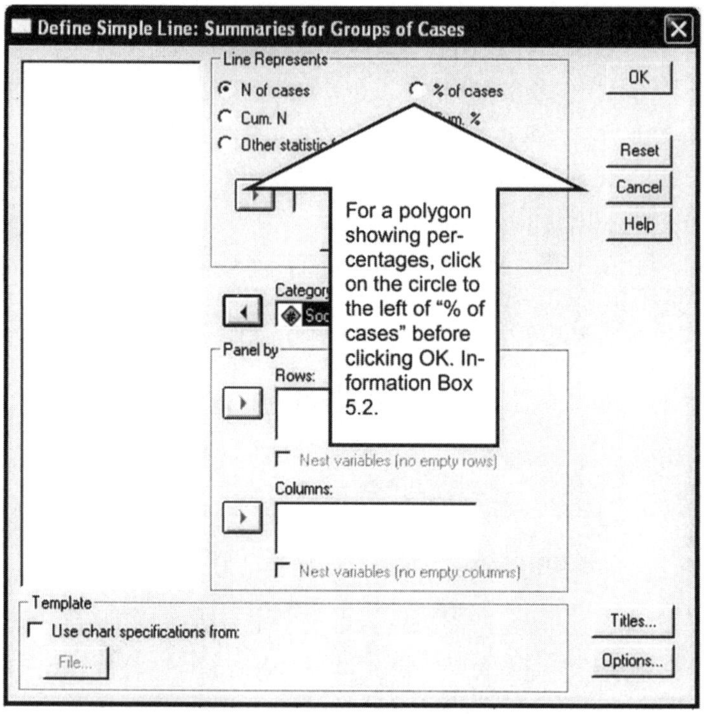

Figure 5.5. See Information Box 5.2 on the previous page.

→ Graph

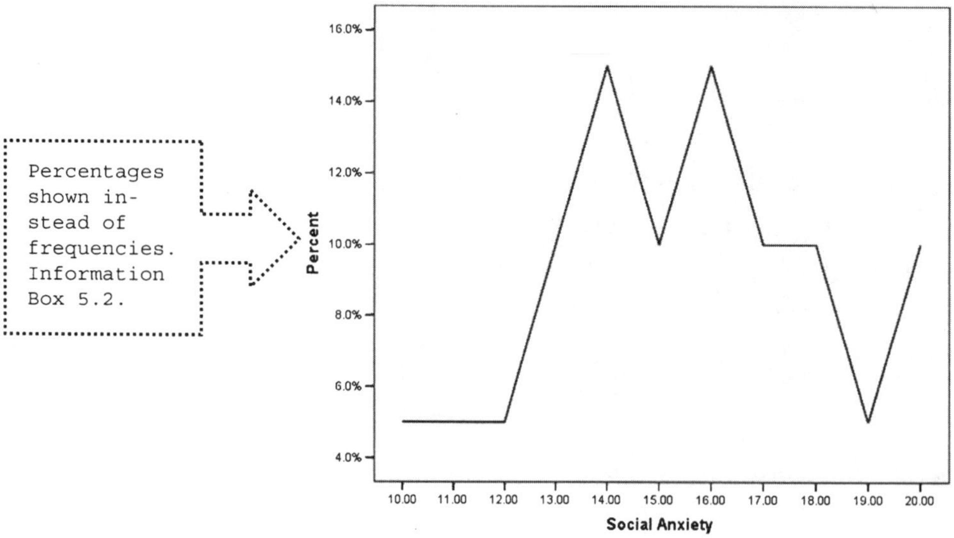

Figure 5.6. Polygon showing percentages for Social Anxiety scores (see Information Box 5.2 on the previous page).

Exercise for Chapter 5

1. Prepare a frequency polygon for the Current Events Knowledge Test scores shown in Table 5.2 below. When you create the data file, name the variable "Current" and label it "Current Events Knowledge." See Chapter 2 for directions for creating a new data file.

Table 5.2

Current Events Knowledge Test Scores on a Scale from 0 to 12 for 20 Students

0	7	1	2	3	5	7	5	10	6
8	9	5	6	4	5	7	6	11	12

2. Prepare a polygon showing *percentages* for the scores on the ABC Depression Inventory shown in Table 5.3 below. When you create the data file, name the variable "Depression" and label it "Depression Scores." See Chapter 2 for directions on creating a new data file.

Table 5.3

ABC Depression Inventory Scores on a Scale from 10 to 20 for 20 Clients

17	18	19	20	13	13	14	14	15	16
15	10	11	12	16	17	18	15	16	14

Notes:

Chapter 6

Mean, Median, and Mode:
One Group, Two Scale Variables

***Learning objectives*:**
1. Define the three measures of central tendency (i.e., mean, median, and mode).
2. Identify when to use the mean, median, and mode.
3. Distinguish between the meanings of line numbers in the Variable View and Data View modes.
4. Calculate the mean and median using SPSS.
5. Identify the mode in a frequency distribution.
6. Present the mean and median in a research report.
   a. Select the appropriate symbol for the mean.
   b. Determine the number of decimal places to use when reporting the mean and median.

Definition of "Mean," "Median," and "Mode"

The "mean," "median," and "mode" are members of a family of statistics known as *measures of central tendency* (i.e., types of *averages*).

The *mean* is defined as *the balancing point in a distribution of scores*. It is calculated by summing all the scores and dividing by the number of scores.

The *median* is defined as *the middle point in a distribution of scores*. It is calculated by arranging the scores in order from high to low and counting to the middle score, which is the median.

The *mode* is defined as *the most frequently occurring score in a distribution*. For instance, if more participants have a score of 10 than any other score, then 10 is the mode.

When to Use the Mean, Median, and Mode

By far, the *mean* is the most frequently used measure of central tendency in published research. Its use is appropriate for describing the average of a distribution of scores when the following two conditions are met:

a. the distribution of scores is *not* highly skewed[1], ***and***

b. the scores are at the *scale* (i.e., interval or ratio) level of measurement.[2]

The *median* is an alternative to the mean. The median is appropriate for use when:

a. the distribution of scores is highly skewed, making the mean inappropriate, ***or***

b. the scores are at the *ordinal* level of measurement, making the mean inappropriate.

The *mode* is sometimes reported in conjunction with either the mean or median in order to provide consumers of research with an additional perspective on the average of a distribution of scores. However, its use in published research is very rare.[3]

Calculating the Mean and Median Using SPSS

Step 1: Start SPSS by clicking on "Start" at the lower-left corner of the screen, and then clicking on "SPSS for Windows."[4]

After executing Step 1, you should see the dialog box shown in ***Figure 6.1 on the next page***. By default, SPSS assumes you will be opening an existing data source (notice the circle with a dot in it in Figure 6.1 on the next page). Because you will be entering new data (instead of working with some data that was previously saved), follow the next step.

Step 2: Click on the circle to the left of "Type in data," and then click OK.

See the arrows in Figure 6.1 on the next page.

---

[1] A *skewed* distribution is one in which there are extreme scores at one end of the distribution but not at the other. An example of such a distribution is shown later in this chapter. Note that the normal bell-shaped distribution is the most common type of symmetrical distribution.

[2] See Chapter 1 to review levels of measurement.

[3] Its use is rare because it has two weaknesses: (1) a given distribution can have more than one mode, while there is only one mean and median for a given distribution and (2) for reasons that are beyond the scope of this book, the mode is less reliable than the mean or median for estimating the average of a population based on a random sample from the population.

[4] You may have to first click on "All Programs" to get a list of programs from which you can select "SPSS for Windows."

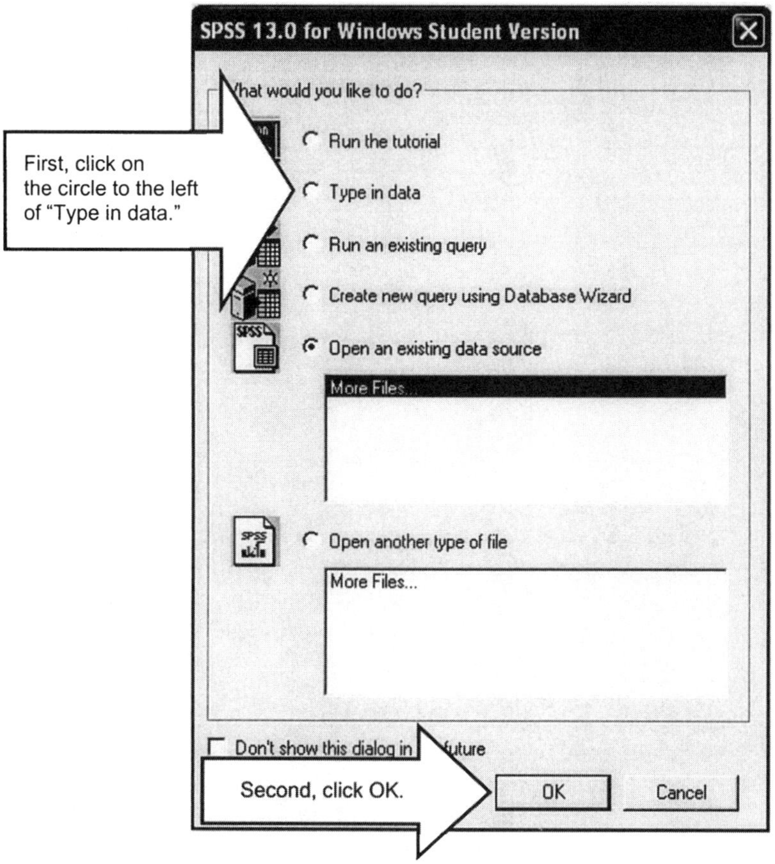

Figure 6.1. Sequence for Step 2.

Step 3: Click on "Variable View" to be sure you are in the Variable View screen.

See Figure 6.2 on the next page.

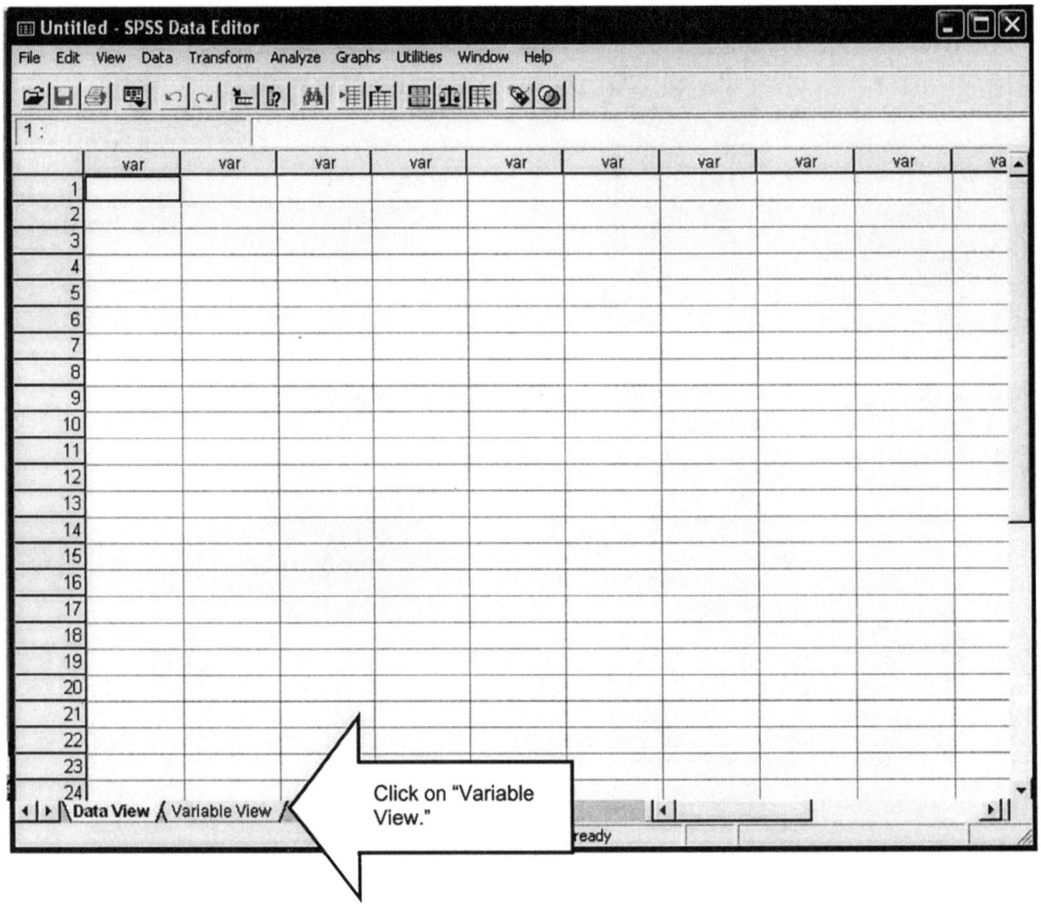

Figure 6.2. Step 3.

Note that scores on an Attitude Toward Tobacco scale with possible scores ranging from 0 to 10 will be entered. To give this variable a brief name, follow the next step.

Step 4: Name the variable by typing the word "Tobacco."

By default, SPSS will put whatever you first type when you first enter the Variable View mode into the first cell near the upper-left corner of the screen just under the word "Name." *See the arrow for Step 4 in Figure 6.3 on the next page*.

Step 5: Click on the empty cell just below the word "Label," and type the words "Attitude Toward Tobacco."[5]

After executing Step 5, you should see the words you typed in the cell under the word "Label." *See the arrow for Step 5 in Figure 6.3 on the next page.*

---

[5] You can also move to the cell under the word "Label" by repeatedly pressing the Tab key on the keyboard.

Step 6: Click on the "Data View" tab at the lower-left corner of the Data Editor.

See the arrow for Step 6 in Figure 6.3 below.

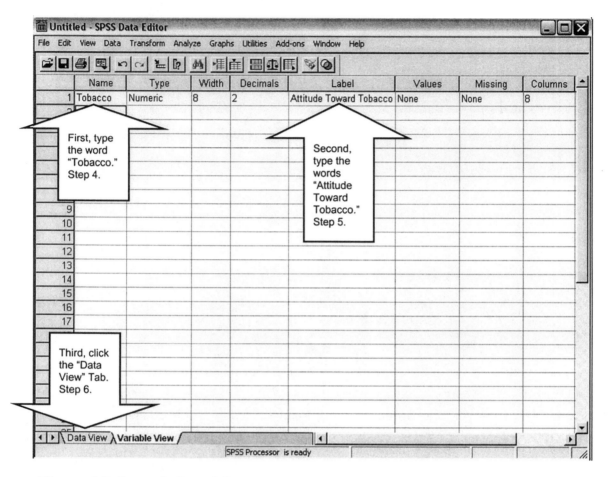

Figure 6.3. Steps 4, 5, and 6.

Figure 6.4 on the next page shows what the screen will look like after you execute Step 6. You will be in the Data View screen, which allows you to enter data.

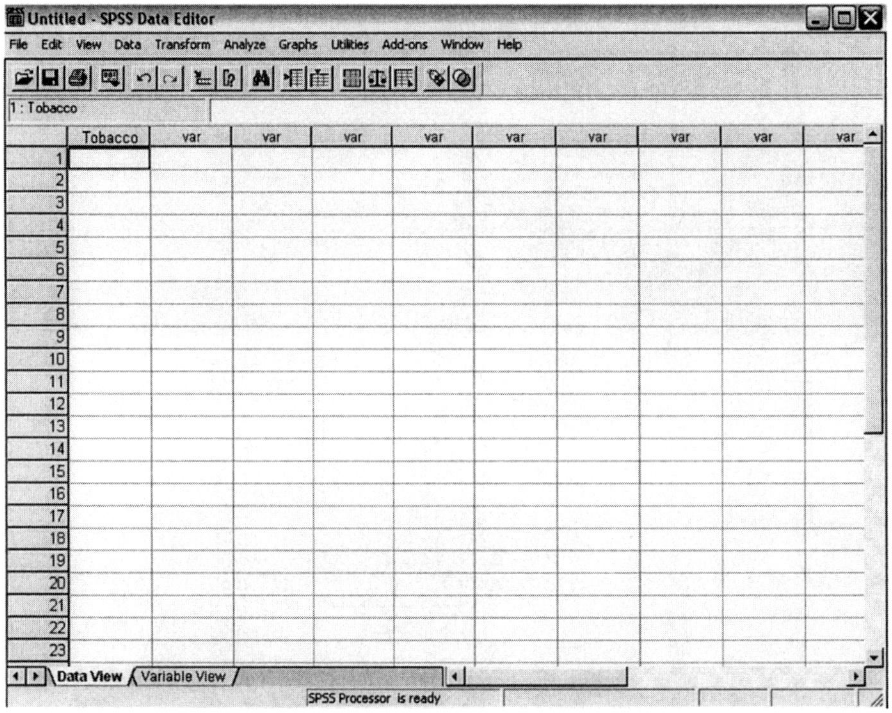

Figure 6.4. The Data View screen produced by Step 6.

Before proceeding to the next step, consider the Attitude Toward Tobacco scores in Table 6.1 below. The scores were obtained using a scale that presents ten positive statements regarding tobacco (i.e., "People who smoke tobacco look sophisticated."). For each statement, each of the 20 students in a stop-smoking class checked "yes" or "no." For each "yes," a participant obtained a score of "1." Then, these scores were summed to get a total score for each participant. Thus, a score of 6 indicates that the participant checked "yes" for six of the ten positive statements about tobacco. Obviously, the scores can range from zero to ten. Like scores on a multiple-choice test, these scores are assumed to be at the *interval* (i.e., *scale*) level of measurement (see Chapter 1 to review levels of measurement).

Table 6.1
Attitude Toward Tobacco Scores on a Scale from 0 to 10 for 20 Students in a Stop-Smoking Class

9	8	4	6	5	7	8	3	2	1
1	7	6	5	8	4	5	6	3	8

Step 7: Type the number "9" (the first score in Table 6.1 above), and then press the Tab, Enter, or down-arrow key on the keyboard. Then, type the remaining scores (8, 4, 6, etc.), remembering to press the Tab, Enter, or down-arrow key after typing each one.

Note that the numbers from 1 to 20 in the first column are participant numbers (in this case, Participants 1 through 20). After executing Step 7, the scores will be in the second column. *Figure 6.5 below shows the Data View screen with the scores entered.*

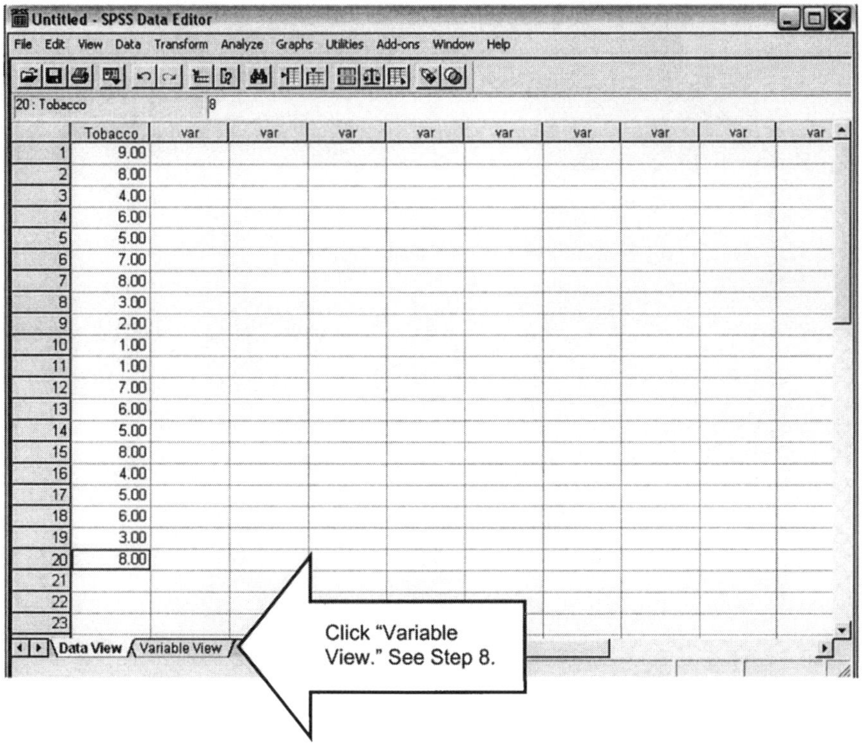

Figure 6.5. The Data View screen after all the scores are entered in Step 7. Also, see Step 8.

Step 8: Click on the Variable View tab.

See the arrow in Figure 6.5 above.

By executing Step 8, you will be returning to the "Variable View" screen because you will be entering the data for a second variable to the data file. These data consist of the self-reported number of cigarettes smoked the previous day by individuals who just enrolled in a stop-smoking class. They are shown in Table 6.2 on the next page.

Step 9: Give the second variable the name "Cigarettes" and the label "Number of Cigarettes Smoked."

Enter this information on row 2. *See the arrows for Step 9 in Figure 6.6 on the next page.*

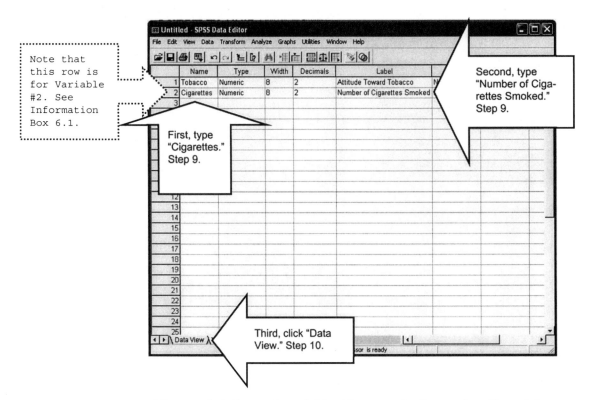

Figure 6.6. Steps 9 and 10. Also, see Information Box 6.1 below.

Information Box 6.1

Meaning of Line Numbers in the Variable View Mode

In the Variable View mode, each line number represents a separate variable. In Figure 6.6 above, Line Number 1 contains the variable labeled "Attitude Toward Tobacco." In the same figure, Line Number 2 contains the variable labeled "Number of Cigarettes Smoked."

Step 10: Click on the Data View tab, and then enter the scores for Number of Cigarettes Smoked from Table 6.2 below.

Table 6.2

Number of Cigarettes Smoked on the Previous Day by Individuals in a Stop-Smoking Class

52	8	10	15	20	18	62	21	15	17
16	25	8	12	10	14	15	16	8	48

See Figure 6.7 on the next page, which shows the scores for both variables after they have been entered into SPSS.

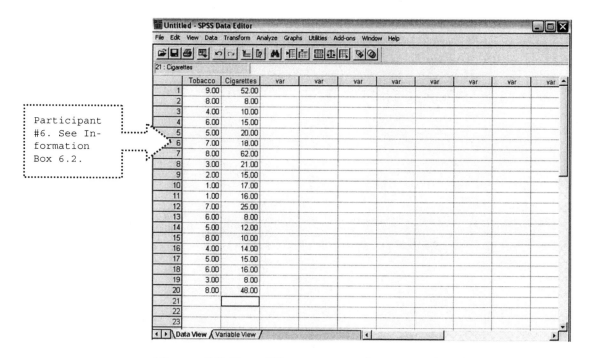

Participant #6. See Information Box 6.2.

Figure 6.7. Data View screen after executing Step 10. See Information Box 6.2 below.

Information Box 6.2

Meaning of Line Numbers in the Data View Mode

In the Data View mode, each line number represents an individual participant. For instance, Participant Number 6 has an Attitude Toward Tobacco score of 7 and a Number of Cigarettes Smoked score of 18. ***See the arrow in Figure 6.7 above***.

Step 11: Name and save the data file.

To execute this step, click on "File" near the upper-left corner of the screen, then click on "Save As," and then type "Tobacco and Cigarettes" as the file name.

Step 12: Click on "Analyze."

See the arrow for Step 12 in Figure 6.8 on the next page.

Step 13: Move the cursor to "Descriptive Statistics."

When you execute Step 13, another drop-down menu will appear. ***See the arrow for Step 13 in Figure 6.8 on the next page***.

Step 14: Click on "Explore...."

See the arrow for Step 14 in Figure 6.8 below.

As a result of executing Step 14, you will see the dialog box in Figure 6.9 on the next page.

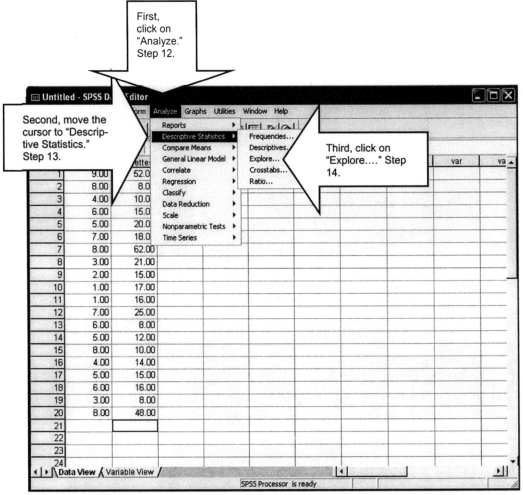

Figure 6.8. Steps 12, 13, and 14.

Step 15: Select "Attitude Toward Tobacco" for analysis.

Note that by default, SPSS highlights the first variable in the list, which in this case is "Attitude Toward Tobacco." It is highlighted with a blue background.

To select "Attitude Toward Tobacco" for analysis, click on the top arrowhead, which will move "Attitude Toward Tobacco" from the list of variables to the "Dependent List" on the right. ***See the arrow for Step 15 in Figure 6.9 on the next page.***

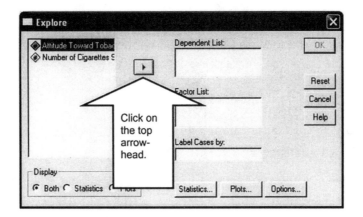

Figure 6.9. Step 15.

Step 16: Also, select "Number of Cigarettes Smoked" for analysis.

To execute this step, first click on the name of the variable ("Number of Cigarettes Smoked"),[6] and then click on the top arrowhead. ***See the arrows for Step 16 in Figure 6.10 below***.

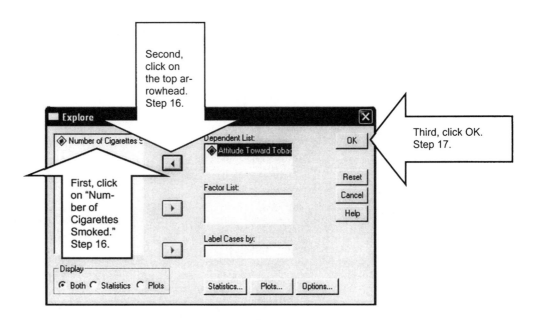

Figure 6.10. Sequence for Step 16. Also, Step 17.

Step 17: Click on OK.

See the arrow for Step 17 in Figure 6.10 above.

---

[6] Clicking on "Number of Cigarettes Smoked" will highlight it. Once it is highlighted, the arrowhead will turn to point to the right.

After clicking OK, the SPSS output will be displayed. Scroll through it until you find the box that reports the means and medians for the two variables. ***See Table 6.3 below for the SPSS output***.

Table 6.3

Portion of the Output Showing the Means and Medians for "Attitude Toward Tobacco" and "Number of Cigarettes Smoked"

				Statistic	Std. Error
Attitude Toward Tobacco	Mean	Mean = 5.3000		5.3000	.54338
	95% Confidence Interval for Mean			4.1627	
		Upper Bound		6.4373	
	5% Trimmed Mean			5.3333	
	Median			5.5000	
	Variance			.95	
	Std. Deviation		Median = 5.5000		
	Minimum				
	Maximum				
	Range			8.00	
	Interquartile Range			4.50	
	Skewness			-.340	.512
	Kurtosis			-.885	.992
Number of Cigarettes Smoked	Mean	Mean = 20.5000		20.5000	3.42014
	95% Confidence Interval for Mean			13.3416	
		Upper Bound		27.6584	
	5% Trimmed Mean			18.8889	
	Median			15.5000	
	Variance			47	
	Std. Deviation		Median = 15.5000		
	Minimum				
	Maximum				
	Range			54.00	
	Interquartile Range			10.25	
	Skewness			1.860	.512
	Kurtosis			2.574	.992

(Variable Number 1)

(Variable Number 2)

Step 18: Save and close the output.

Click on "File" near the upper-left corner of the screen and then click on "Save As." Give the data file the name "Tobacco and Cigarettes Output," and click on "Save" near the lower-right corner of the dialog box. Then, click the red box with the arrow at the top right of the screen to close the output screen.

Identifying the Mode in a Frequency Distribution

The *mode* (the most frequently occurring score) is rarely reported in published research, and is not identified by SPSS in the output shown in Table 6.3 on the previous page.

In a distribution with a small number of scores, it is sometimes easy to spot without the assistance of SPSS. For instance, consider again the Attitude Toward Tobacco scores analyzed earlier in this chapter, which are shown again in Table 6.4 below. In it, the score of 8 occurs more often than any other score, so the mode for this distribution is 8.

Table 6.4
Attitude Toward Tobacco Scores with the Mode of 8 (the Most Frequently Occurring Score)
Shown in Bold

9	**8**	4	6	5	7	**8**	3	2	1
1	7	6	5	**8**	4	5	6	3	**8**

With a large number of scores in a distribution (such as dozens or more scores), SPSS can be used to facilitate identification of the mode by using it to prepare a frequency distribution (as illustrated in Chapter 3). If you prepare one for the scores in Table 6.4 above, you will obtain the output shown in Table 6.5 below. In this frequency distribution, you can see that a score of 8 has the highest frequency (4), so 8 is the mode. (Obviously, the values in the first column of Table 6.5 are the scores from 1 through 9.)

Table 6.5
Frequency Distribution for "Attitude Toward Tobacco," with the
Mode Being the Score with the Highest Frequency

		Frequency	Percent	Valid Percent	Cumulative Percent
Valid	1.00	2	10.0	10.0	10.0
	2.00	1	5.0	5.0	15.0
	3.00	2	10.0	10.0	25.0
	4.00	2	10.0	10.0	35.0
	5.00	3	15.0	15.0	50.0
	6.00	3	15.0	15.0	65.0
	7.00	2	10.		75.0
	8.00	4			95.0
	9.00	1	5.		100.0
	Total	20	100.0	100.0	

The mode is 8.

The highest frequency is 4.

Selecting Between the Mean and Median for a Research Report

Selecting an Average for a Highly Skewed Distribution

In a *skewed distribution*, there are some extremely low or high scores that are not counterbalanced by extremes at the other side. For instance, the distribution of Number of Cigarettes Smoked is clearly skewed. The scores (i.e., number smoked) are presented again in Table 6.6 below. As you can see, the scores in bold (52, 62, and 48) are atypical of the group because they are very high. In addition, there are no very low scores (such as minus 48 [–48]) to balance the distribution at the low end.

Table 6.6

Number of Cigarettes Smoked with Extremely High Scores that Skew the Distribution Shown in Bold

52	8	10	15	20	18	**62**	21	15	17
16	25	6	12	10	14	15	16	8	**48**

When a distribution is highly skewed, the values of the mean and median will be noticeably different because the mean (but not the median) will be pulled toward the extreme scores. For instance, the value of the mean for Number of Cigarettes Smoked in Table 6.3 on page 60 is 20.50. In contrast, the median is only 15.50, which is more typical of the majority of the group of students. (More of the students have scores that are near 15 than scores that are near 20.) Because the median is more typical than the mean, the median should be presented in a research report.

Selecting an Average for a Distribution That Is Not Highly Skewed

Assuming that a variable is at the scale level (i.e., interval or ratio) *and* the distribution is not highly skewed, the mean is the type of average almost all researchers would select for presentation in a research report.

Presenting the Mean and Median in a Research Report

As you know from the material near the beginning of this chapter, the mean is appropriate for describing the average for a *scale variable* (i.e., interval or ratio variable). However, it is inappropriate for describing the average of a distribution that is highly skewed. The following material illustrates this principle. Specifically, the median can be substituted for the mean when a distribution is highly skewed.

Presenting the Median for a Highly Skewed Distribution

For a highly skewed distribution, do one of two things.

a. Present the median without presenting the mean (see Example 6.1 below), *or*

b. present the median *and* also present the mean for additional information for readers of research reports (see Example 6.2 below).

Example 6.1

Statement that presents the median for a highly skewed distribution.

"The distribution of number of cigarettes smoked is highly skewed with only three of the 20 students reporting that they smoked 48 or more cigarettes on the previous day. The median number smoked was approximately 15 (*mdn* = 15.50)."

Example 6.2

Statement that presents the median *and* mean for a highly skewed distribution.

"The distribution of number of cigarettes smoked is highly skewed with only three of the 20 students reporting that they smoked 48 or more cigarettes on the previous day. The median number smoked was approximately 15 (*mdn* = 15.50). Because the distribution is highly skewed to the right, the mean (*M* = 20.50) is higher than the median."

Information Box 6.3

Symbols for the Mean in Research Reports

> The uppercase, italicized letter *M* is the appropriate symbol for the mean when an entire population has been studied (such as all patients in a hospital ward when the researcher wants to describe *only* these patients).
>
> The lowercase, italicized letter *m* is the symbol for the mean when only a sample from a population has been studied (such as a random sample of 50% of the patients in a hospital when the researcher wants to generalize to all patients in the hospital).
>
> Authors of many statistics textbooks use the symbol X-bar ($\overline{X}$) as the symbol for the mean. However, this symbol is very rarely used in published research reports.

Presenting the Mean for a Distribution That Is Not Highly Skewed

If a distribution is *not* highly skewed, the mean is the preferred statistic for describing the average of a distribution for a scale variable (i.e., interval or ratio variable). The symbols for presenting the mean are discussed in Information Box 6.3 above.

A mean can be presented in a sentence, as in Example 6.3 below. Note that the sentence does not mention whether the distribution is skewed, so the reader of the research will have to assume that it is not skewed. It is conventional to omit mention of whether a distribution is skewed when the mean (without the median) is presented in published research reports.

Example 6.3
Statement that presents the mean for a distribution that is not highly skewed.

"Attitude Toward Tobacco for 20 students who were starting a stop-smoking class was measured on a self-report scale with possible scores from 0 to 10. The mean score was 5.30."

Information Box 6.4
Number of Decimal Places to Report for the Mean and Median

The general rule of thumb in statistical reporting is to report statistics to two more decimal places than existed in the original data. For instance, the scores on all scale variables in this book are whole numbers. Therefore, reporting statistics such as the mean and median to two decimal places (i.e., $M = 5.30$) is appropriate for these data.

Note that when a mean is reported, the standard deviation (a statistic discussed in the next topic) is nearly always reported, as well. Also, note that when there are a number of means (either because there are a number of variables and/or a number of groups for which means have been calculated), the means and standard deviations are often reported in statistical tables, which is illustrated in the next topic.

Exercise for Chapter 6

1. You will be entering the scores shown in Table 6.7 below (for "Number of Hours Using the Internet") into SPSS. In the Variable View mode, name this variable "Hours" and label it "Hours Using Internet." Then, enter the scores in order (22, 1, 0, etc.) in the Data View mode. ***See Steps 1 through 8 in this chapter***.

Table 6.7
Number of Hours College Students Used the Internet for Course-Related Information in a Week

22	1	0	3	1	2	3	4	5	1
4	3	1	0	2	3	0	33	2	25

2. *In the same data file as you entered the Number of Hours Using the Internet*, you will also be entering the scores shown in Table 6.8 below (for "Attitude Toward Internet Use") into SPSS. First, in the Variable View mode, *name* this variable "Internet" and *label* it "Attitude Toward Internet." ***See Steps 8 through 10 in this chapter***.

Table 6.8
Attitude Toward Internet Use for Information for Coursework on a Scale from 0 to 10

10	7	3	4	3	5	6	7	6	1
7	5	3	4	6	5	7	6	4	9

3. Save the data file using the name "Internet Hours and Attitude." (Click on "File," then "Save As," then name the file and click "Save." ***See Step 11 in this chapter***.)

4. Use SPSS to calculate the mean and median for each of the two variables. ***See Steps 12 through 18 in this chapter***.

    a. What is the mean for "Hours Using Internet"? _____

    b. What is the median for "Hours Using Internet"? _____

    c. Would you report "the mean" *or* "the median" *or* both "the mean and median" in a research report for "Hours Using Internet"? _____

        Explain: _____

    d. Write a statement that presents one or both of the averages for "Hours Using Internet":

        _____

    e. What is the mean for "Attitude Toward Internet"? _____

    f. What is the median for "Attitude Toward Internet"? _____

    g. Would you report "the mean" *or* "the median" *or* both "the mean and median" in a research report for "Attitude Toward Internet"? _____

        Explain: _____

    h. Write a statement that presents one or both of the averages for "Attitude Toward Internet":

        _____

        _____

        _____

        _____

Notes:

Chapter 7

Mean and Standard Deviation:
Two or More Groups, One Scale Variable

***Learning objectives*:**

1. Review the definition of the mean.
2. Define the standard deviation.
3. Identify when to use the mean and standard deviation.
4. Identify when to use the median and interquartile range.
5. Enter data consisting of codes for group membership and scores for a scale variable.
6. Identify independent and dependent variables for analysis by SPSS.
7. Calculate the means and standard deviations separately for each group.
8. Present means and standard deviations in a research report.
   a. Present means and standard deviations within a sentence.
   b. Present means and standard deviations in a statistical table.

Definition of "Mean" and "Standard Deviation"

As you know from the previous chapter, the *mean* is defined as *the balancing point in a distribution of scores*. It is calculated by summing all the scores and dividing by the number of scores.

The *standard deviation* is defined as *the number of score points out from the mean of a normal distribution that includes 34% of the cases*.[1] If a distribution is only approximately normal, the percentage will vary.

While the mean is a measure of central tendency (i.e., a type of average), the standard deviation is a measure of *variability*, which refers to the extent to which the scores vary (i.e., differ) from each other. For instance, if all the scores in a distribution are the same (e.g., all participants have a score of 10), there is no variability and the standard deviation will equal 0.00. To the extent that the scores differ from each other, the standard deviation will increase in size.

---

[1] Technically, the standard deviation is defined as the number of score points from the mean of a normal (bell-shaped) distribution to the point where the slope of the normal curve changes direction (a point known as the point of inflection). If a distribution is normal, by definition, 34% of the cases lie between the mean and one standard deviation unit from the mean.

When to Use the Mean and Standard Deviation

When it is appropriate to use the mean to describe the average of a distribution of scores, the standard deviation should be used to describe the variability of the distribution. As you know from the previous chapter, it is appropriate to use the mean when:

a. the distribution of scores is *not* skewed[2], **and**

b. the scores are at the *scale* (i.e., interval or ratio) level of measurement.[3]

Information Box 7.1

The Median and the Interquartile Range As Alternatives to the Mean and Standard Deviation

> As you know from the previous chapter, the *median* is the average that is the middle point in a distribution. The *median* is an alternative to the mean. The median is appropriate for use when:
>
> a. the distribution of scores is highly skewed, *or*
>
> b. the scores are at the *ordinal* level of measurement.
>
> When the median is selected as the appropriate measure of central tendency for a distribution, the *interquartile range* (*not* the standard deviation) is the appropriate measure of variability for that distribution.
>
> The interquartile range is defined as the range of scores for the middle 50% of a distribution. It is a modification of the simple range, which is the number of score points covered from the lowest to the highest scores.
>
> Examine again the output in Table 6.3 on page 60 in Chapter 6. You will see both the median and interquartile range reported by SPSS for each variable in that example.

Assigning Numerical Codes to Identify Groups

You will be entering the data in Table 7.1 on the next page into SPSS. Note that there are two variables in the table. The first variable is "Dosage Level" of a drug (low, moderate, and high). For analysis by SPSS, you will use the following codes, as shown in the table: 1 = low, 2 = moderate, and 3 = high. Thus, the codes 1, 2, and 3 will identify the members of each group.

The second variable is "Reported Pain Level," which is the amount of pain reported by the participants one hour after receiving a dose of the pain-relieving drug. Pain was reported on a 10-point scale from 0 (no pain) to 10 (extreme pain).

---

[2] A *skewed* distribution is one in which there are extreme scores at one end of the distribution but not at the other. An example of such a distribution (number of cigarettes smoked) was shown in the previous chapter (see the scores in Table 6.6 on page 62 in Chapter 6). Note that the normal bell-shaped distribution is the most common type of symmetrical (nonskewed) distribution.

[3] See Chapter 1 to review levels of measurement in more detail.

Table 7.1

Dosage Level and Reported Amount of Pain Data for Nine Participants

Participant number	Dosage level	Codes for dosage levels	Reported pain level
1	High	3	3
2	Moderate	2	5
3	Low	1	7
4	Low	1	8
5	High	3	2
6	High	3	1
7	Moderate	2	8
8	Moderate	2	4
9	Low	1	6

Calculating Means and Standard Deviations

Step 1: Click on "Variable View," name the first variable "Dosage," and label it "Dosage Level."

See the arrows for Step 1 in Figure 7.1 on the next page.

Step 2: Click on "Values."

See the arrow for Step 2 in Figure 7.1 on the next page.

Step 3: Click on the small gray box that will appear under "Values" after executing Step 2.

See the arrow for Step 3 in Figure 7.1 on the next page.

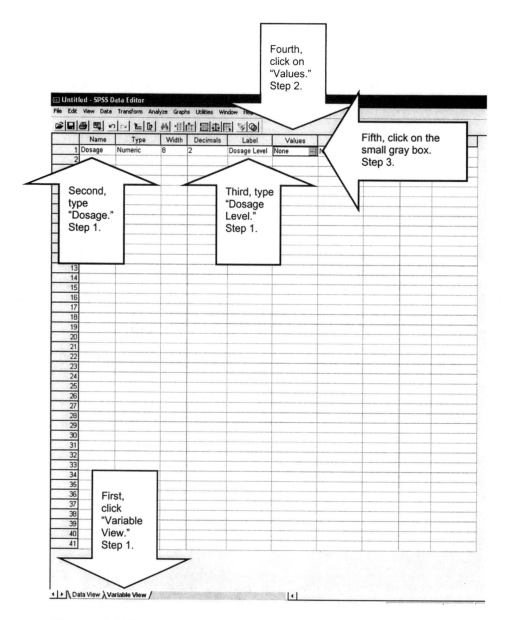

Figure 7.1. Steps 1, 2, and 3.

Step 4: Type the number "1" in the space to the right of the word "Value" in the dialog box.

After executing Step 3, the dialog box shown in Figure 7.2 on the next page will appear. Type the number "1" in the space for "Value" in this dialog box.

See the arrow for Step 4 in Figure 7.2 on the next page.

Step 5: Type the words "Low Dosage" in the space to the right of the words "Value Label."

By executing Steps 4 and 5, you are indicating that the number 1 is the code (i.e., called the "value" in SPSS) for Low Dosage. Do *not* type the quotation marks; SPSS will automatically add them after Step 6. *See the arrow for Step 5 in Figure 7.2 below.*

Step 6: Click "Add."

See the arrow for Step 6 in Figure 7.2 below.

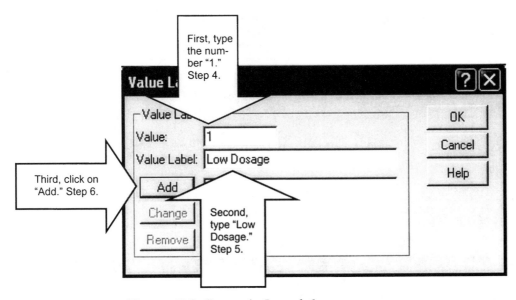

Figure 7.2. Steps 4, 5, and 6.

Step 7: Repeat Steps 4 through 6, using the Value of "2" and the Value Label "Moderate Dosage."

Be sure to click "Add." Do not click OK yet.

Step 8: Repeat Steps 4 through 6, using the Value of "3" and the Value Label "High Dosage."

Figure 7.3 on the next page shows what the Value Labels dialog box should look like after completing Steps 6 through 8.

Step 9: Click OK.

See Figure 7.3 on the next page.

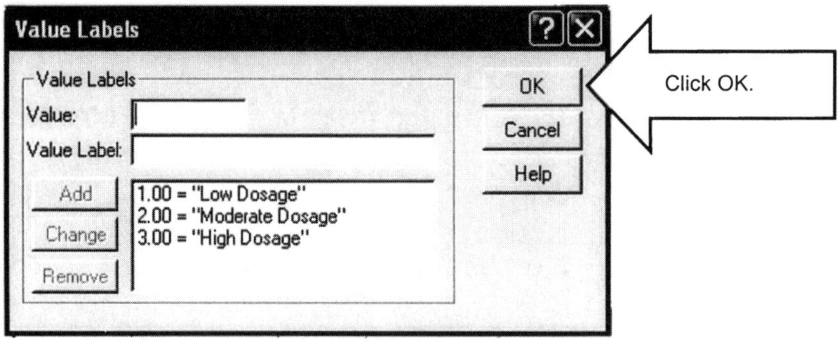

Figure 7.3. Value Labels dialog box after values have been entered for three levels of dosage to identify groups. Also, see Step 9.

After executing Step 9, SPSS will return to the Variable View screen.

Step 10: Name the second variable "Pain," and label it "Reported Pain Level." *See Figure 7.4 below.*

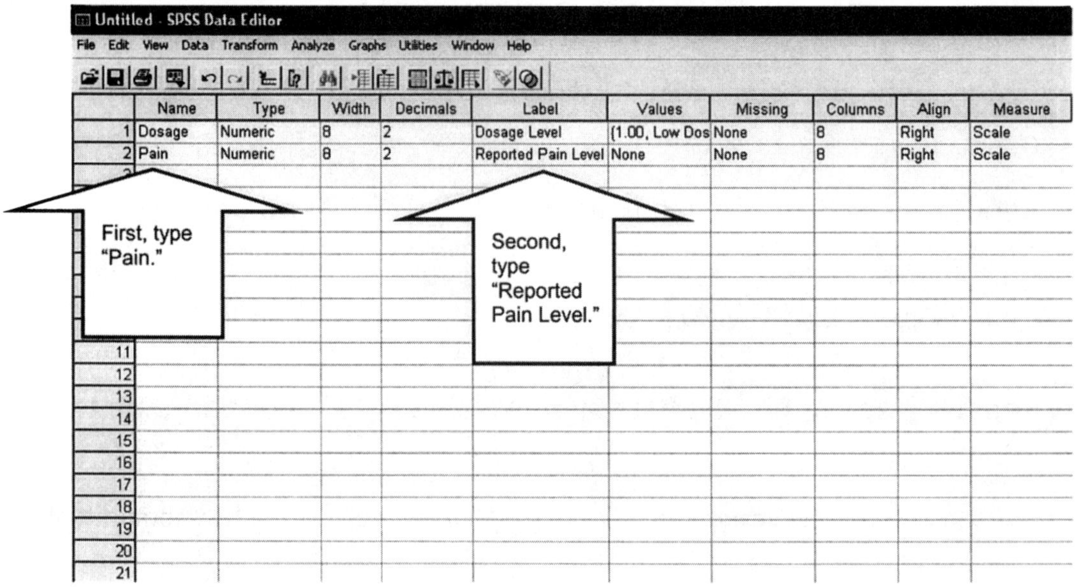

Figure 7.4. Sequence for Step 10.

Step 11: Click on the "Data View" tab, and enter the scores for the two variables.

For Dosage Level, use the codes 1, 2, and 3 (*not* the words low, moderate, and high). **Figure 7.5 on the next page** shows the Data View screen after the scores for the two variables have been entered. Remember to press the Enter or down-arrow key after entering the last score for reported pain level (the score of 6).

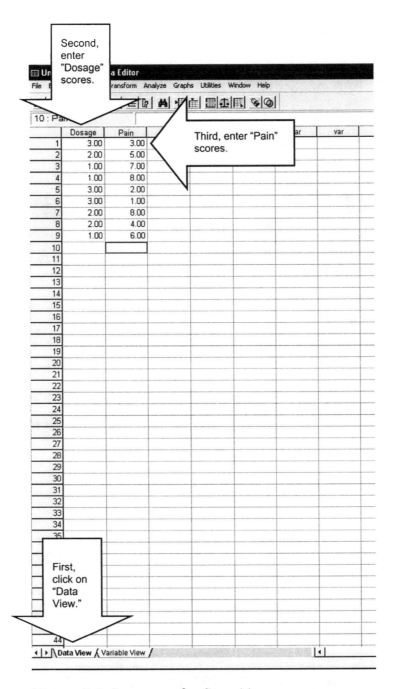

Figure 7.5. Sequence for Step 11.

Step 12: Name and save the data file.

To execute this step, click on "File" near the upper-left corner of the screen. Next, click on "Save As," then type "Dosage and Pain" as the file name. You will be using this file in Chapter 14.

Step 13: Click "Analyze," then put the cursor on "Compare Means," and then click "Means...."

See Figure 7.6 below.

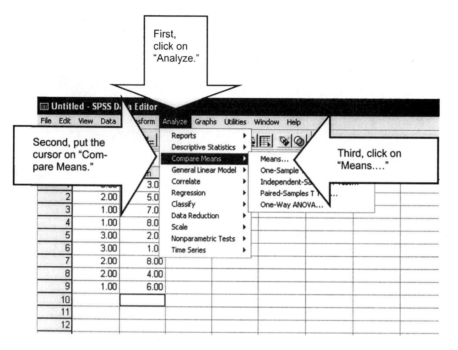

Figure 7.6. Sequence for Step 13.

After executing Step 13, the "Means..." dialog box will appear on the screen.

Step 14: Click on the bottom arrowhead for the "Independent List."

In the dialog box, the variable labeled "Dosage Level" will be highlighted in blue. Move it to the Independent List by clicking on the bottom arrowhead.

See Figure 7.7 below.

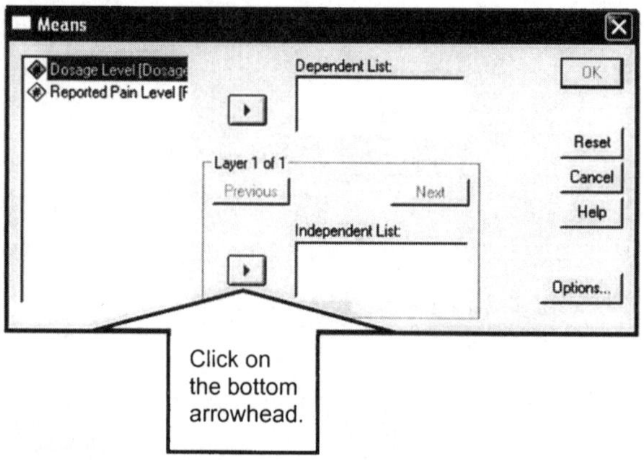

Figure 7.7. Step 14.

Information Box 7.2

Distinguishing Between Independent and Dependent Variables in SPSS

In Step 14, you moved the variable labeled "Dosage Level" into the "Independent List" in the "Means…" dialog box (see Figure 7.7 on the previous page). An *independent variable* is a categorical variable that identifies group membership. In the example being considered in this chapter, the independent variable is "Dosage Level," which identifies these three groups: (a) low dosage group, (b) moderate dosage group, and (c) high dosage group. An *independent variable* is sometimes called the *input variable* or *stimulus variable*.

In Step 15, you will move the variable labeled "Reported Pain Level" into the "Dependent List" in the "Means…" dialog box (see Figure 7.8 below). A dependent variable is the outcome associated with the independent variable. In the example being considered in this chapter, the dependent variable is "Reported Pain Level," which might be associated with and possibly influenced by the independent variable. Thus, the Dosage Level (the independent variable) might influence the Reported Pain Level (the dependent variable). A *dependent variable* is sometimes called the *outcome variable* or *response variable*.

Step 15: Click on the label "Reported Pain Level," and then click on the top arrowhead for the "Dependent List."

Clicking on "Reported Pain Level" will select it (with blue highlight). Move it to the Dependent List by clicking on the arrowhead.

See Figure 7.8 below.

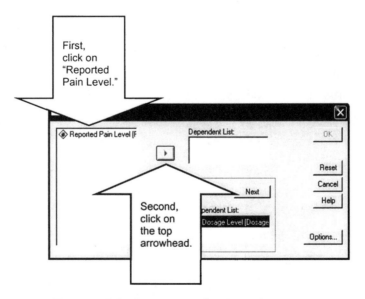

Figure 7.8. Sequence for Step 15.

Step 16: Click OK.

See Figure 7.9 below.

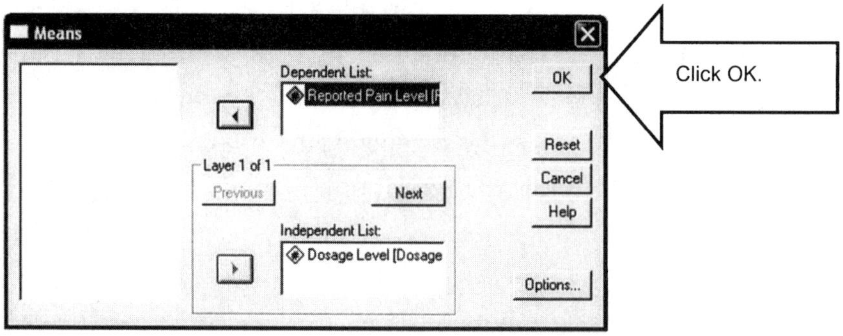

Figure 7.9. Step 16.

After executing Step 16, the SPSS output shown in Table 7.2 below will appear on your screen.

Table 7.2
Means and Standard Deviations (Unformatted SPSS Output)

Reported Pain Level

Dosage Level	Mean	N	Std. Deviation
Low Dosage	7.0000	3	1.00000
Moderate Dosage	5.6667	3	2.08167
High Dosage	2.0000	3	1.00000
Total	4.8889	9	2.57121

Interpreting the SPSS Output

Examining the means in Table 7.2 above, it is clear that the mean for High Dosage (2.0000) is substantially lower than the means for Moderate Dosage (5.6667) and Low Dosage (7.0000). Thus, those who received the highest dosage reported the least amount of pain. Also, there was more variability for the Moderate Dosage group (as indicated by a standard deviation of 2.08167) than for the other two groups, each of which has a standard deviation of 1.00000.

Note that the letter "N" is shown in the output. "N" is used by SPSS to indicate the number of cases (3 in each group and 9 in all).

Presenting Means and Standard Deviations in a Research Report

Presenting Means and Standard Deviations Within a Sentence

The three means and standard deviations can be reported within a sentence as illustrated in Example 7.1 on the next page.

Example 7.1

Means and standard deviations presented within a sentence.

"On a scale from 0 (no pain) to 10 (extreme pain), the group that received the high dosage reported less pain (*m* = 2.00, *sd* = 1.00, *n* = 3) than the moderate dosage group (*m* = 5.67, *sd* = 2.08, *n* = 3) and the low dosage group (*m* = 7.00, *sd* = 1.00, *n* = 3)."

Note three characteristics of the sentence presenting the results in Example 7.1 above:

a. The symbols for the mean (*m*), standard deviation (*s*), and the number of cases (*n)* are italicized, which is standard in statistical reporting.[4]

b. The lowercase *m* stands for the mean for a sample drawn from a population, and the lowercase *s* stands for the standard deviation for a sample drawn from a population. The lowercase *n* stands for the number of cases in the sample. If an entire population had been studied, the uppercase symbols *M*, *S*, and *N* should be used.

c. The results were rounded to two decimal places (e.g., the mean of 5.6667 was rounded to 5.67). When the raw data consist of whole numbers (such as the pain scores), it is traditional to round the statistical results to two places for presentation in research reports.

Presenting Means and Standard Deviations in a Statistical Table

Reporting means and standard deviations in a statistical table can help readers make comparisons across groups of participants. The SPSS output in Table 7.2 on the previous page is formatted in Table 7.3 below to be consistent with the style suggested in the *Publication Manual of the American Psychological Association.*

Table 7.3

Means and Standard Deviations of Pain Scores for Three Dosage Levels

Dosage level	Mean	Standard deviation
High (*n* = 3)	2.00	1.00
Moderate (*n* = 3)	5.67	2.08
Low (*n* = 3)	7.00	1.00

Note. Pain measured on a scale from 0 (no pain) to 10 (extreme pain). The higher the score, the more pain.

---

[4] Some researchers use *sd* as the symbol for the standard deviation. Authors of statistics textbooks often use symbols other than *m* and *s*. However, in published research in the social and behavioral sciences, the symbols *m* and *s* (either uppercase or lowercase) are standard.

Exercise for Chapter 7

You will be analyzing the data in Table 7.4 below. Follow the steps in this chapter to obtain the means and standard deviations for the three groups. Then, present the means and standard deviations in a sentence appropriate for inclusion in a research report (see Example 7.1 on the previous page). Finally, prepare a table showing the statistics (see Table 7.3 on the previous page for a sample table). In the Variable View mode, name the first variable "SES" and label it "Socioeconomic Level." While still in the Variable View mode, name the second variable "Savings" and label it "Dollars in Savings Accounts." Note that Socioeconomic Level is the independent variable, and Dollars in Savings Accounts is the dependent variable.

Table 7.4

Socioeconomic Level and Dollars in Savings for 12 Participants

Participant Number	Socioeconomic Level (SES)	Codes for SES	Dollars in Savings Accounts
1	High	3	30,000
2	Medium	2	20,000
3	Low	1	2,000
4	High	3	10,000
5	Medium	2	12,000
6	Low	1	1,000
7	High	3	5,000
8	Medium	2	9,000
9	Low	1	5,000
10	High	3	14,000
11	Medium	2	12,000
12	Low	1	6,000

Chapter 8

Z-Scores (Standard Scores)

Learning objectives:
1. Define the terms "z-score," "standard score," and "standardized values."
2. Calculate z-scores for individuals in a group.
3. Interpret z-scores.
4. Identify uses for z-scores.

Definition of "Z-Score"

A z-score is a score expressed in standard deviation units. The scores usually range from −3.00 to 3.00[1]. Here are the meanings of selected z-scores.

    a. A z-score of 0.00 indicates that a participant has the same score as the average participant in a group.

    b. A z-score of 1.00 indicates that a participant has the same score as a participant who is one standard deviation *above* the mean.

    c. A z-score of −2.00 indicates that a participant has the same score as a participant who is two standard deviations *below* the mean.

As you may have surmised from the above examples, a z-score with a positive value indicates that a participant is above the average (i.e., above the mean), while a z-score with a negative value indicates that a participant is below the average.

As you consider the examples in this chapter, the meaning of z-scores will be clearer.

Information Box 8.1

Alternative Terminology: Standard Score, Standardized Value (SPSS Terminology)

    Authors of statistics textbooks invariably use the term *z-score* to refer to the type of score defined at the beginning of this chapter.

    Some authors use *standard score* as a synonym for *z-score*.

    SPSS also uses the term *z-score*, but as you will see later in this chapter, SPSS also refers to *z-scores* as *standardized values*.

---

[1] In a normal distribution, only part of one percent of the cases lie above a z-score of 3.00. Thus, z-scores above 3.00 are very rare. Likewise, scores below −3.00 are very rare.

Computing *Z*-Scores Using SPSS

Table 8.1 below contains the number-correct scores on a math test and a reading test taken by one group of participants. The math test contains 20 test items (with the possible scores from 0 to 20), while the reading test contains 40 test items (with the possible scores from 0 to 40). As you can see, comparing scores across tests to determine strengths and weaknesses of individual participants is difficult because the two tests contain different numbers of test items, resulting in different ranges of possible scores.[2] In fact, all the reading scores are higher than any of the math scores, which might be due merely to the fact that there were more test items on the reading test than on the math test. Using z-scores will "correct" for this possibility.

Table 8.1

Number-Correct Scores on a Math Test and a Reading Test
for One Group of Participants

Participant number	Math	Reading
1	4	24
2	6	26
3	8	28
4	10	30
5	12	32
6	14	34
7	16	36

Step 1: Click on "Variable View," name the first variable "Math," and name the second variable "Reading."

First, click on the Variable View tab to make sure you are in the Variable View mode. Then, name the two variables. (It is not necessary to label the variables for the activities in this chapter.) ***See the arrows for Step 1 in Figure 8.1 on the next page.***

---

[2] Even if the two tests had the same number of items, the comparison for the purpose of determining whether a participant was stronger in one area (such as math) than another (such as reading) would be confounded because the two tests might vary in difficulty. For instance, the math test might contain relatively *difficult* math items while the reading test might contain relatively *easy* reading items. Thus, if *both* tests contained 10 items and a participant marked 5 items correctly on both tests, it would not be clear whether the participant is equally strong in both areas. Using z-scores (both of which are based on the mean and standard deviation of a single group), it is possible to make a legitimate comparison across subject matter areas such as math and reading, as illustrated later in this chapter.

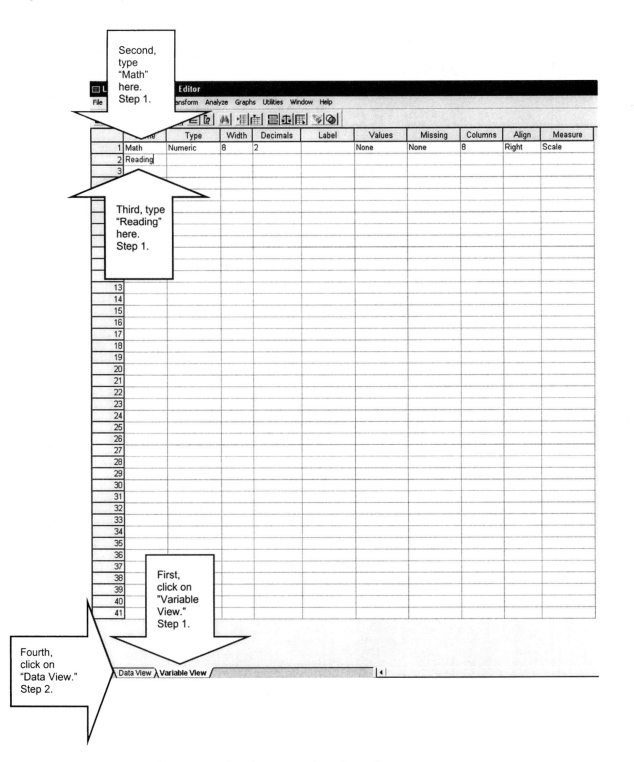

Figure 8.1. Sequence for Step 1. Also, Step 2.

Step 2: Click on the "Data View" tab.

See the arrow for Step 2 in Figure 8.1 above.

Step 3: Enter the data for the two variables from Table 8.1 page 80.

See the data in Figure 8.2 below.

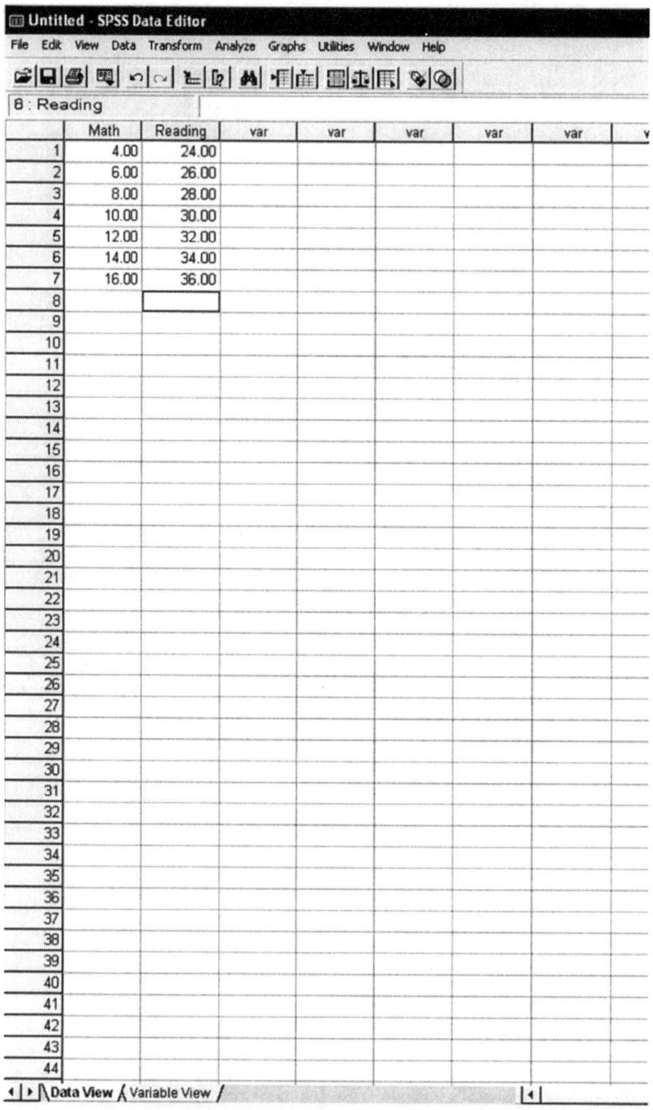

Figure 8.2. The Data View screen after the scores have been entered.

Step 4: Click on "Analyze," then move the cursor to "Descriptive Statistics," and then click on "Descriptives...."

See Figure 8.3 on the next page.

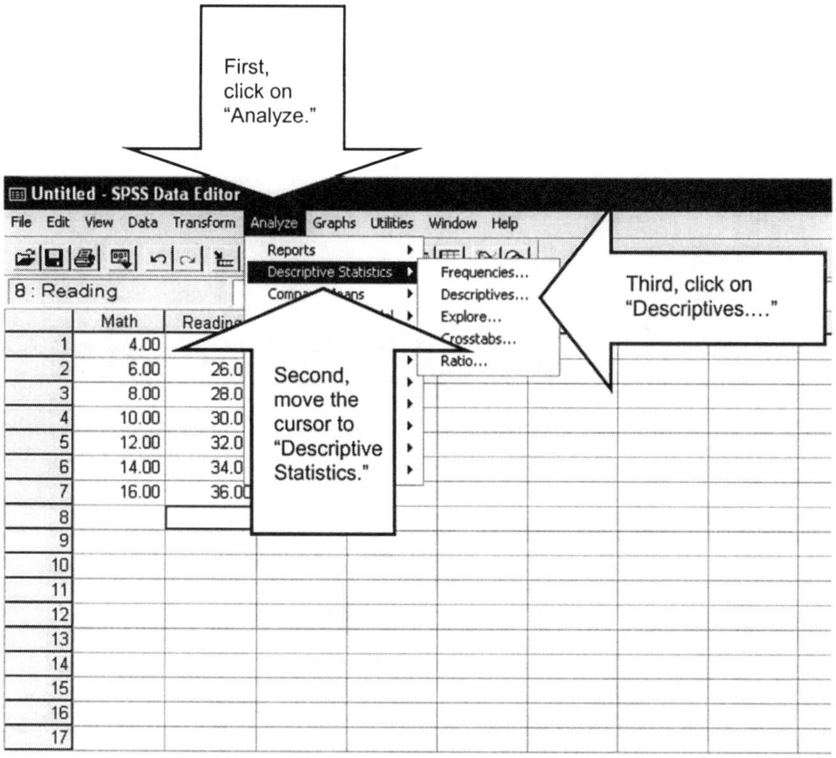

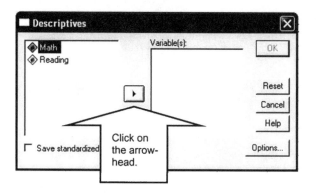

Figure 8.3. Sequence for Step 4.

After executing Step 4, the "Descriptives…" dialog box will appear on the screen.

Step 5: Move "Math" to the "Variable(s)" box by clicking on the arrowhead.

Note that the variable(s) placed in the "Variable(s)" box are the variable(s) that SPSS will analyze. ***See Figure 8.4 below.***

Figure 8.4. Step 5.

Step 6: Move "Reading" to the "Variable(s)" box by first clicking on the word "Reading" and then clicking on the arrowhead.

See Figure 8.5 below.

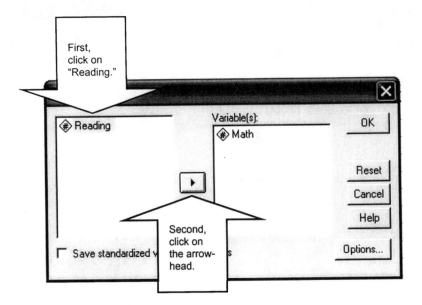

Figure 8.5. Sequence for Step 6.

Step 7: Click on the small box to the left of "Save standardized values as variables."

When you click on it, a check mark will appear in the box. *See the arrow for Step 7 in Figure 8.6 below.*

Step 8: Click OK.

See the arrow for Step 8 in Figure 8.6 below.

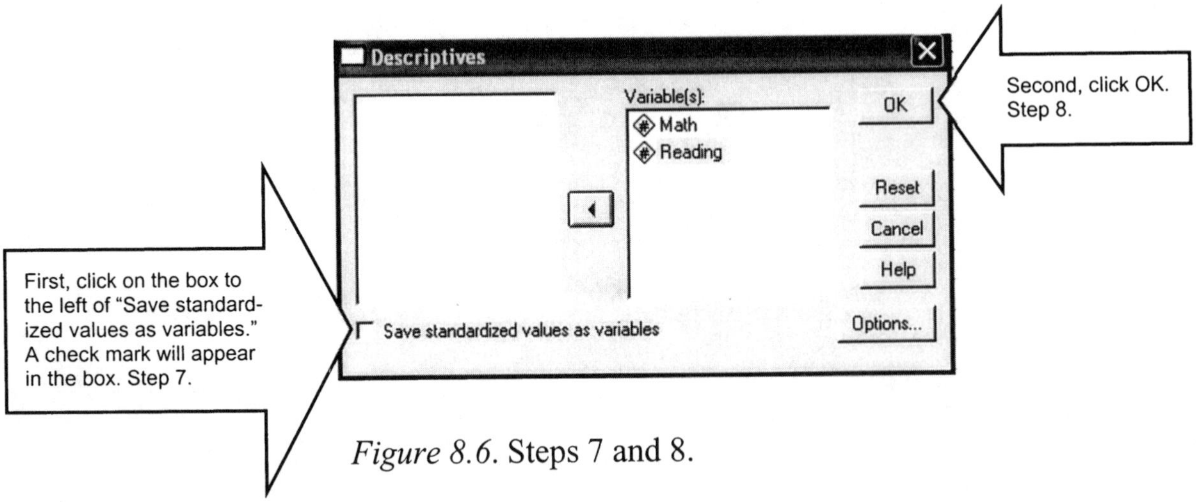

Figure 8.6. Steps 7 and 8.

After executing Step 8, SPSS will produce the output (with means and standard deviations) shown in Figure 8.7 below.

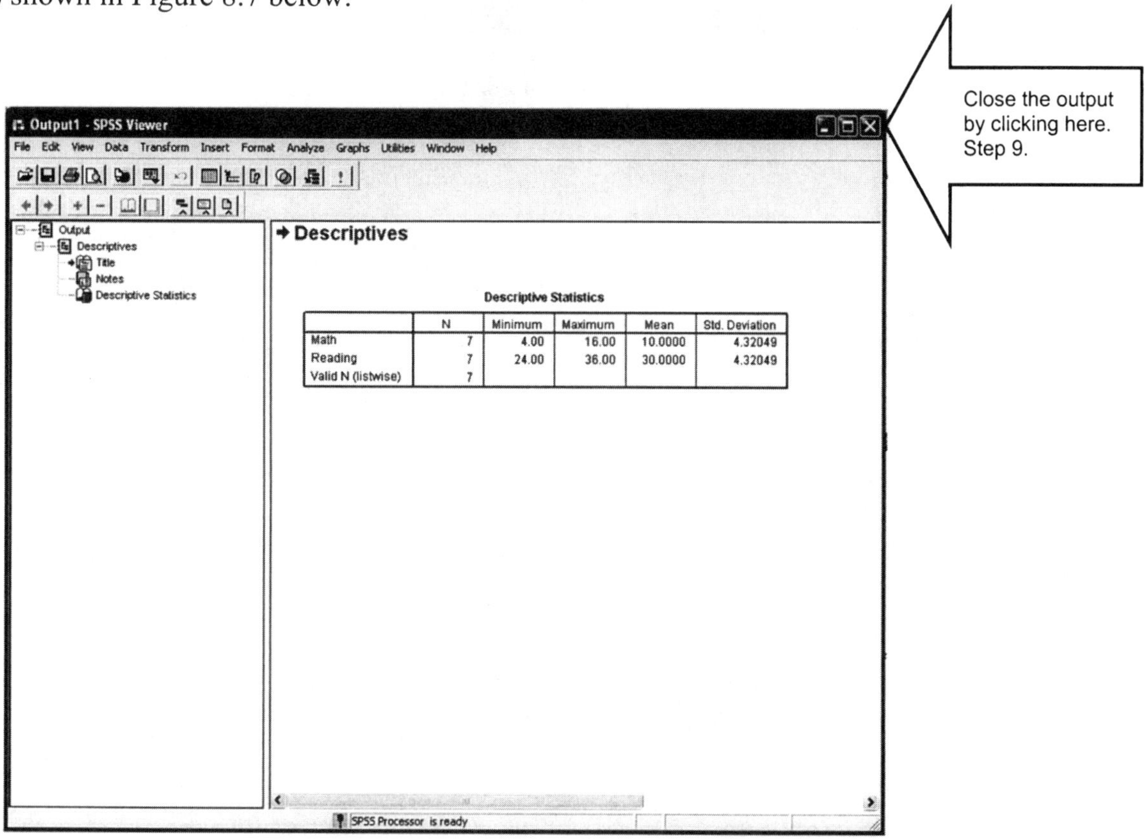

Figure 8.7. Output for number-correct scores after executing Step 8. Also, see Step 9.

Step 9: Close the output by clicking on the small red box with the X in it near the upper right of the screen (*or* by clicking on "File" near the upper left of the screen and then "Close").

See the arrow for Step 9 in Figure 8.7 above.

After you execute Step 9, SPSS will give you the opportunity to save the output. It is not necessary to do so for the purposes of this example.

After you have closed the output, you will be able to see that SPSS has added two new variables to the Data View screen, which are shown in *Figure 8.8 on the next page*. They are the *z*-scores for math and the *z*-scores for reading.

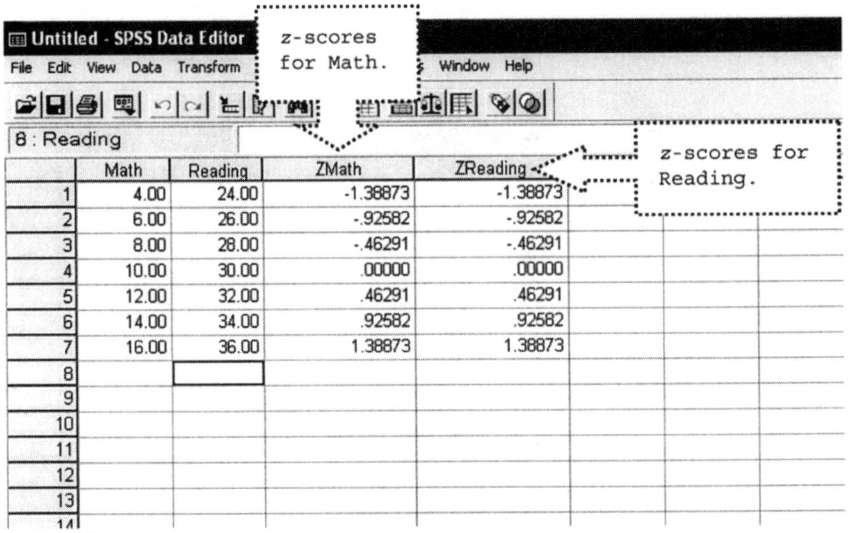

Figure 8.8. Z-scores for Math and the *z*-scores for Reading revealed after closing the output screen in Step 9.

Interpreting *Z*-Scores

Interpreting *Z*-Scores That Equal Zero

In the original data (see Table 8.1 on page 80), it superficially appears that Participant Number 4 is stronger in reading (with a number-correct score of 30) than in math (with a number-correct score of 10). However, in Figure 8.8 above, you can see that Participant Number 4 has a *z*-score of zero (0.00000) in *both* reading and math. These *z*-scores indicate that Participant Number 4 is exactly average (at the mean) on both tests. Thus, the appropriate interpretation is that Participant Number 4 is average in both areas and is *not* stronger in one area than the other.

It is important to note that any participant who has a number-correct score that is exactly the same as the mean score of the group will have a *z*-score of zero. In addition, any participant who has a *z*-score that is close to zero is, by definition, close to the average of the group.

Interpreting *Z*-Scores That Are Positive in Value

In Figure 8.8 above, you can see that Participant Number 5 has a *z*-score for math of .46291, which is close to .50. This indicates that this participant is about half a standard deviation *above* the mean of the group. *A z-score with a positive value indicates that a participant is above the mean of the group.*

Interpreting *Z*-Scores That Are Negative in Value

In Figure 8.8 above, you can see that Participant Number 1 has a *z*-score for math of −1.38873, which is close to −1.50. This indicates that this participant is about one and a half standard deviations *below* the mean of the group. *A z-score with a negative value indicates that a participant is below the mean of the group.*

Interpreting *Z*-Scores in Light of the Normal Curve

In a normal distribution, 34% of the cases lie between a *z*-score of 0.00 and 1.00, which might be thought of as "high average." Likewise, 34% lie between 0.00 and –1.00, which might be thought of as "low average." Z-scores above 1.00 are very high relative to the group, while *z*-scores below –1.00 are very low relative to the group.

Uses for *Z*-Scores

First, as you saw immediately above, *z*-scores are useful for interpreting the scores of individual participants on one or more tests.

Second, *z*-scores are the basis for the computation of the Pearson product-moment correlation coefficient, a very widely used statistic that is covered in Chapter 10.

Presenting *Z*-Scores in a Research Report

Because quantitative research is almost always concerned with describing *groups* and because *z*-scores describe individuals, *z*-scores (as well as other types of standard scores) are rarely presented in published research. The main exception is when a research report deals with the development of a test and presents norms for the test. In this case, the published research might include what is called a *norms table*. This is simply a table that presents the number-correct scores in order from high to low in the first column and the corresponding *z*-scores in the second column.

Exercise for Chapter 8

You will be analyzing the data in Table 8.2 on the next page. Self-esteem was measured with 30 positive statements about the self (e.g., "I like what I see when I look in the mirror."). For each item marked "yes," a participant received one point. Thus, the raw scores could range from zero to 30. Optimism was also measured with a self-report measure that contained 20 items indicating an optimistic attitude (e.g., "I look forward to each new day."). The raw scores could range from 0 to 20.

Follow the steps in this chapter to obtain the (1) output showing the mean and standard deviation for each variable and (2) *z*-scores for both variables. Print the output showing the means and standard deviations as well as the output showing the *z*-scores. Then, answer the questions on the next page.

Note that SPSS will not permit the use of a hyphen when naming a variable nor will it permit the use of two words in a name. Thus, name the first variable "Esteem."

Table 8.2

Raw Scores on a Self-Esteem Scale and an Optimism Scale for One Group of Participants

Participant number	Self-esteem	Optimism
1	30	17
2	27	19
3	25	15
4	22	14
5	19	16
6	17	10
7	16	12
8	15	11
9	15	12

1. What is the z-score on Optimism for Participant Number 3? _____

2. Which participant is exactly at the mean (i.e., exactly average) on Optimism? What is the z-score for this participant? _____

3. How many participants have negative z-scores on Self-Esteem? _____

4. On Self-Esteem, which participant is furthest from the mean? _____
   What is his or her z-score? _____

Chapter 9

Scattergram

Learning objectives:
1. Define the term "scattergram."
2. Identify when to use a scattergram.
3. Create a scattergram using SPSS.
4. Interpret a scattergram in terms of:
    a. strength,
    b. direction, and
    c. linearity.
5. Format a scattergram for presentation in a research report.

Definition of "Scattergram"

A *scattergram* (also known as a *scatter diagram*) is a statistical figure that displays the relationship between two *scale variables* (to review the meaning of this term, see Chapter 1). A scattergram has two axes (one for each variable). The two scores for each participant are represented with a single dot. The pattern of dots indicates the direction and strength of the relationship between the variables. The definition of scattergram will be clearer after you have examined the examples in this chapter.

When to Use a Scattergram

A scattergram should be examined before calculating a correlation coefficient, which is the next topic in this book. The nature of the relationship revealed by a scattergram will help determine which correlation coefficient is appropriate.

Note that a correlation coefficient is a single numerical value used to describe a relationship, while a scattergram is a statistical figure that shows it.

Creating a Scattergram

Step 1: Start SPSS by clicking on "Start" at the lower-left corner of the screen and then clicking on "SPSS for Windows."[1]

After executing Step 1, you should see the dialog box shown in Figure 9.1 on the next page. By default, SPSS assumes you will be opening an existing data source (notice the circle

---

[1] You may have to first click on "All Programs" to get a list of programs from which you can select "SPSS for Windows."

with a dot in it in Figure 9.1 below). Because you will be entering new data (instead of working with some data that were previously saved), follow the next step.

Step 2: Click on the circle to the left of "Type in data," and then click OK.

See Figure 9.1 below.

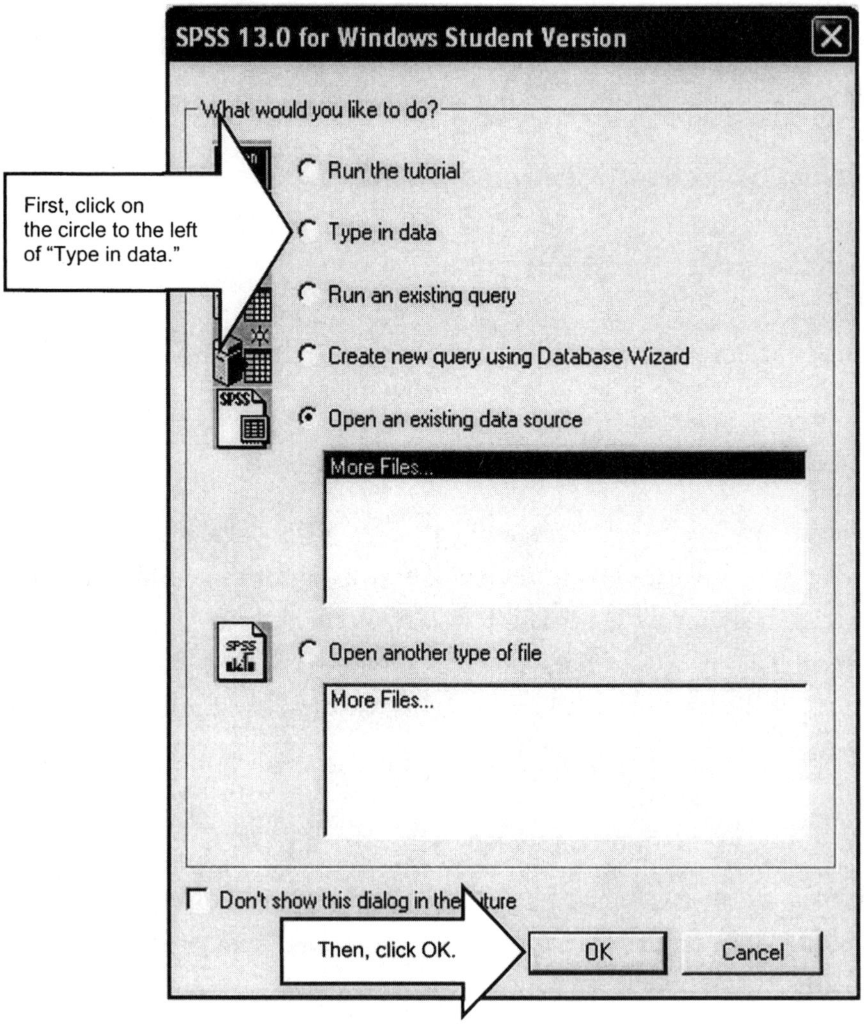

Figure 9.1. Sequence for Step 2.

After executing Step 2, you should see the "SPSS Data Editor" shown in Figure 9.2 on the next page.

Step 3: Click on "Variable View" to be sure you are in the Variable View screen.

See Figure 9.2 on the next page.

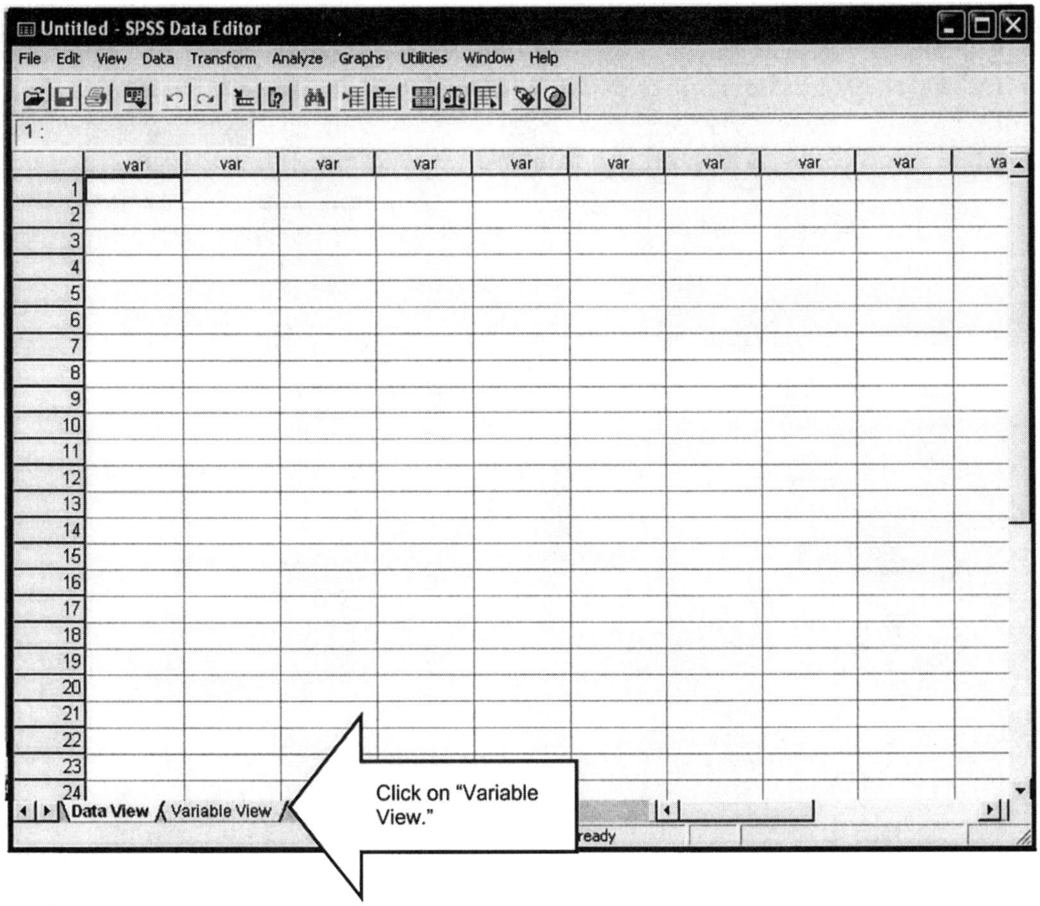

Figure 9.2. Step 3.

In the following steps, you will be entering the participants' scores on the Scholastic Aptitude Test—Verbal (SAT). The scores on the test can range from 200 to 800. Then, you will be entering the same participants' freshmen GPAs. The purpose of the analysis is to determine the relationship between SAT scores and freshmen GPAs (i.e., to determine the extent to which SAT scores predict freshmen GPAs).

Step 4: Name the first variable "SAT," and label it "SAT Verbal Scores."

By default, SPSS will put whatever you first type when you first enter the Variable View mode into the first cell near the upper-left corner of the screen. ***See the arrows for Step 4 in Figure 9.3 on the next page.***

Step 5: Name the second variable "GPA," and label it "Freshmen GPA."

After executing Step 5, you should see the words you typed in the cell under the word "Label." ***See the arrows for Step 5 in Figure 9.3 on the next page.***

Step 6: Click on the "Data View" tab near the lower-left corner.

See the arrow for Step 6 in Figure 9.3 below.

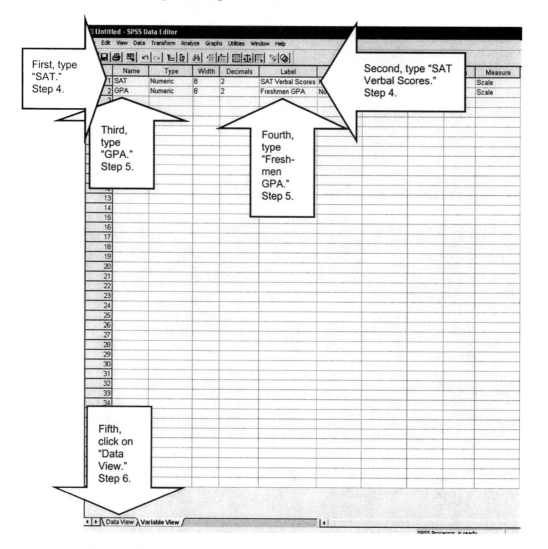

Figure 9.3. Steps 4, 5, and 6.

Step 7: Enter the data for the two variables.

The scores you are to enter are shown in Figure 9.4 on the next page. Note that in the Data View mode, each row represents a single participant. Thus, in Figure 9.4, there are 12 participants with two scores for each participant. *Reminder*: Scattergrams show the relationship between two variables for one group of participants. ***See the scores for Step 7 in Figure 9.4 on the next page.***

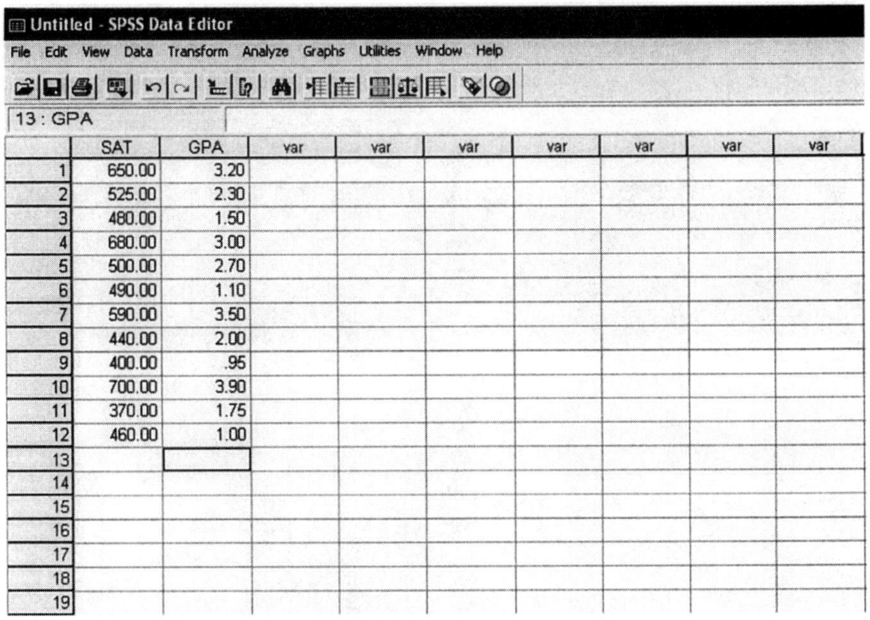

	SAT	GPA	var	var	var	var	var	var	var
1	650.00	3.20							
2	525.00	2.30							
3	480.00	1.50							
4	680.00	3.00							
5	500.00	2.70							
6	490.00	1.10							
7	590.00	3.50							
8	440.00	2.00							
9	400.00	.95							
10	700.00	3.90							
11	370.00	1.75							
12	460.00	1.00							
13									
14									
15									
16									
17									
18									
19									

Figure 9.4. Scores for two variables (one group of participants) to be entered in the Data View mode. The result of executing Step 7.

Step 8: Save the data file with the name "SAT and GPA."

Click on "File" near the upper-left corner of the screen. Then, click on "Save As." Then, type: SAT and GPA. Then, click "Save." *You will need this data file in the next chapter.*

Step 9: Click on "Graphs," and then click on "Scatter/Dot...."

See Figure 9.5 on the next page.

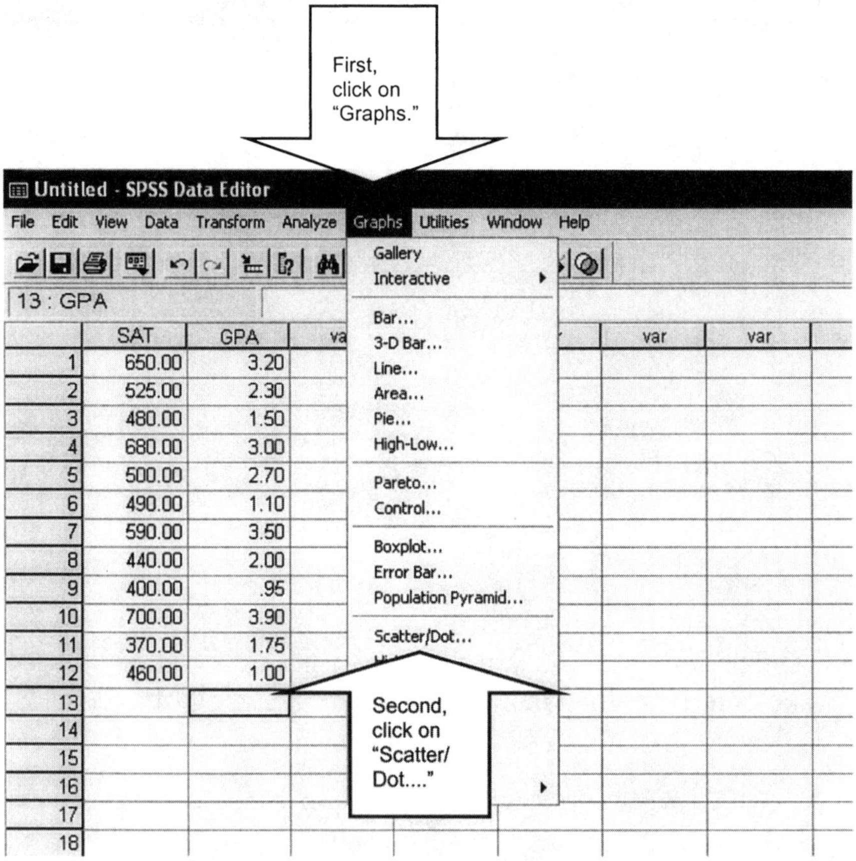

Figure 9.5. Sequence for Step 9.

After executing Step 9, the "Scatter/Dot…" dialog box will appear on the screen.

Step 10: Click on "Define."

By default, SPSS will have already chosen "Simple Scatter" in the dialog box. Because you want to prepare a simple scattergram, simply click on "Define," which will select "Simple Scatter." ***See Figure 9.6 below.***

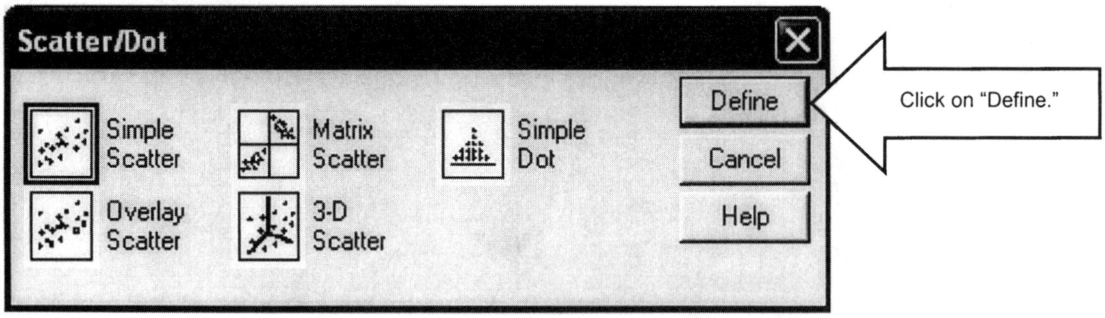

Figure 9.6. Step 10.

Step 11: Click on the arrowhead for the "X Axis."

Note that in Figure 9.7 below, by default SPSS has already selected the first variable in the list ("SAT Verbal Scores"), which is highlighted in blue on the screen. Step 11 will move "SAT Verbal Scores" to the *X* Axis. Also, note that when one variable is intended to predict another, the predictor variable (such as SAT scores) should be named Variable *X*. ***See Figure 9.7 below.***

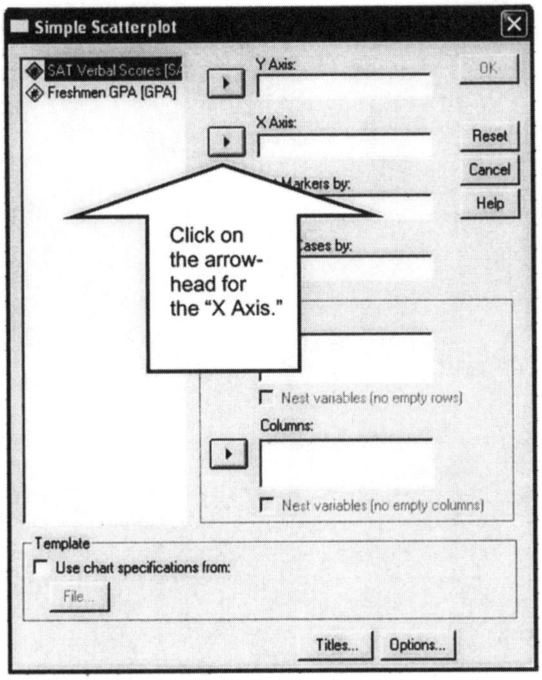

Figure 9.7. Step 11.

Step 12: Click on "Freshmen GPA," and then click on the arrowhead for the "Y Axis."

This step will move "Freshmen GPA" to the *Y* Axis. Note that when one variable is being used to predict another, the variable being predicted (such as GPA) should be named Variable *Y*. Although SPSS does not use the term *criterion*, researchers call the variable being predicted the *criterion variable*. ***See Figure 9.8 on the next page.***

See Information Box 9.1 on page 98 for more information on identifying variables for the *X* and *Y* axes.

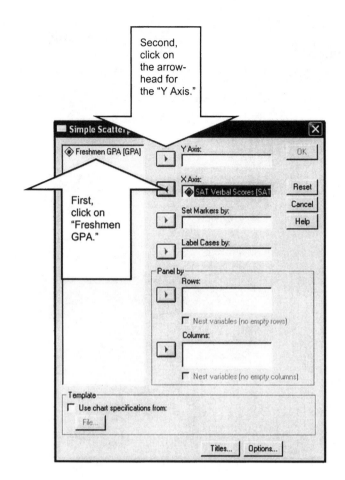

Figure 9.8. Sequence for Step 12.

Step 13: Click OK.

See Figure 9.9 on the next page.

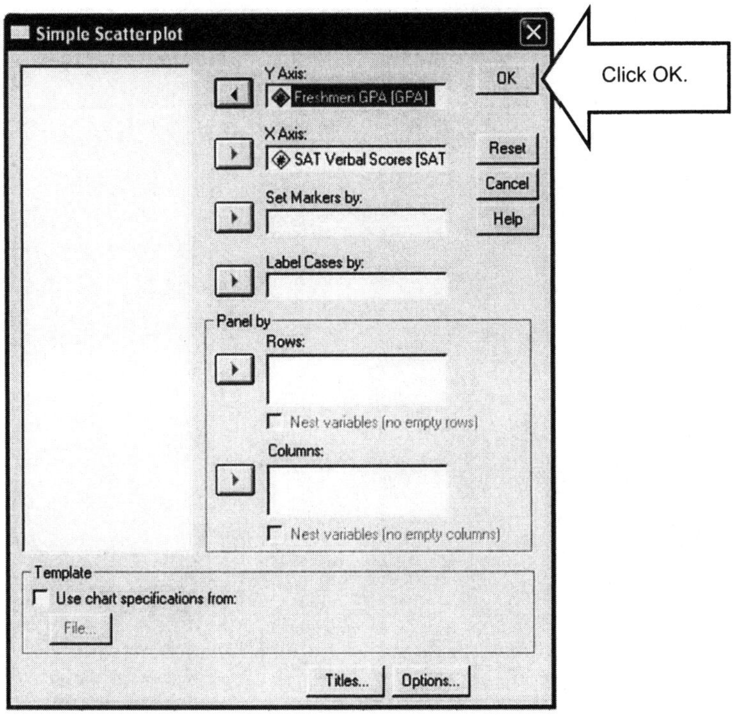

Figure 9.9. Step 13.

After executing Step 13, the scattergram shown in Figure 9.10 on the next page will appear on the screen.

→ Graph

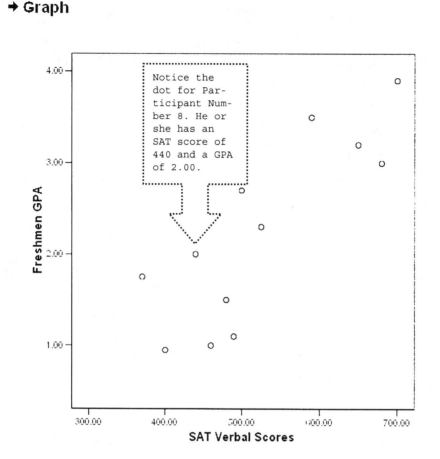

Figure 9.10. Scattergram for the relationship between SAT Verbal Scores and Freshmen GPA (strong, direct, linear relationship).

Information Box 9.1

Identifying Variables for the X and Y Axes in a Scattergram

In statistics in general, the first variable to be measured is identified as variable *X* and the second is identified as variable *Y*. Accordingly, when using a scattergram to examine the predictive abilities of a variable (such as the ability of SAT scores to predict freshmen GPAs), *the predictor variable should be placed on the X axis,* which is the horizontal axis in a scattergram. The variable being predicted (called the outcome or criterion variable) should be placed on the *Y* axis, which is the vertical axis.

While prediction is a major purpose for examining the relationship between two variables, sometimes researchers are interested in the relationship for other reasons such as examining a relationship suggested by a theory. When prediction is *not* involved, it is okay to put either variable on the *X* axis and the other variable on the *Y* axis.

Interpreting the SPSS Output

The scattergram in Figure 9.10 on the previous page has five important characteristics:

1. Each dot on a scattergram represents the *two* scores for *one* participant. For instance, the dot for Participant Number 8 stands for his or her SAT Verbal score of 440 and Freshmen GPA of 2.0. ***See the arrow in Figure 9.10 on the previous page.***

2. As SAT scores increase, GPAs also increase. In other words, those with low SAT scores tend to have low GPAs, while those with high SAT scores tend to have high GPAs. This forms a pattern of dots that rises from the lower-left corner to the upper-right corner. Such a pattern indicates what is called a *positive* or *direct relationship.* (You will see a scattergram for a *negative* or *inverse* relationship later in this chapter.)

3. There is *scatter.* In other words, the dots do *not* form a perfectly straight line but are somewhat scattered. However, the direction of the pattern is clear despite the scatter. The presence of scatter indicates that the relationship is not perfect. (You will see a scattergram for perfect relationship, with no scatter, later in this chapter.)

4. The relationship is *strong.* This is indicated by the fact that the dots are *not* scattered throughout the figure. Instead, they follow a clear pattern. In the next chapter, you will learn about a statistic (a correlation coefficient) that allows you to be specific in determining the strength of relationships.

5. The relationship is *linear.* This means that the dots generally follow a straight line. In the scattergram in Figure 9.10 on the previous page, a single straight line drawn from the lower-left corner to the upper-right corner would clearly indicate the overall pattern of the dots. The fact that the relationship is linear is important because the statistics in the next chapter are designed for describing *linear relationships*. The meaning of a linear relationship will become clearer after you see an example later in this chapter of a *nonlinear* (or *curvilinear*) relationship.

The following are examples of several types of relationships that can be revealed by scattergrams. Considering them will help you in interpreting scattergrams produced by SPSS.

Strong, Direct, Linear Relationship

As you know from the discussion immediately above, the scattergram in Figure 9.10 on the previous page illustrates a strong, direct, linear relationship.

Perfect, Direct, Linear Relationship

In Chapter 8, you saw the scores shown in Figure 9.11 on the next page. The scattergram for these scores is shown in Figure 9.12 on page 101. Because the dots form a single straight line with no scatter of dots around it, the relationship is *perfect*. Also, it is *direct* because the higher the math scores, the higher the reading scores. Obviously, it is also linear because the dots form a straight line.

For extra practice in creating scattergrams, you can use the data in Figure 9.11 below to recreate the scattergram in Figure 9.12 on the next page by following the steps previously described in this chapter.

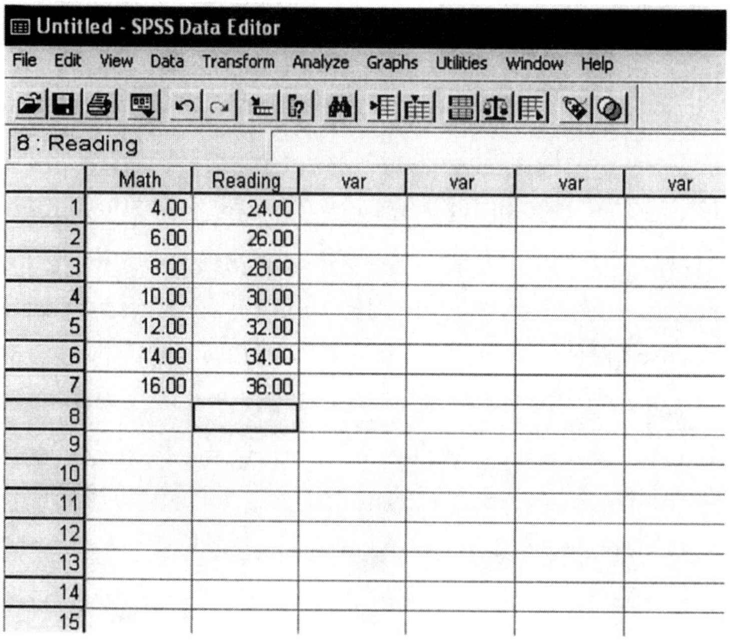

	Math	Reading	var	var	var	var
1	4.00	24.00				
2	6.00	26.00				
3	8.00	28.00				
4	10.00	30.00				
5	12.00	32.00				
6	14.00	34.00				
7	16.00	36.00				
8						
9						
10						
11						
12						
13						
14						
15						

Figure 9.11. Math and Reading scores.

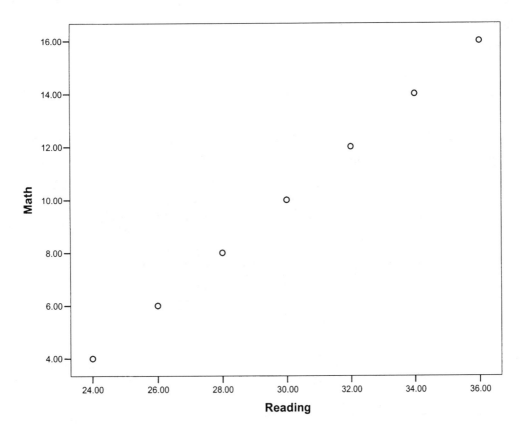

Figure 9.12. Scattergram for the relationship between Reading and Math (perfect, direct, linear relationship).

Strong, Inverse, Linear Relationship

On page 32 in Chapter 4, you saw the scores in Figure 9.13 below. The scattergram for these scores is shown in Figure 9.14 on the next page. The relationship is *inverse* because participants with *better* attitudes toward school have *fewer* days absent. This creates an inverse pattern of dots, going from the upper left to the lower right of the scattergram.

For extra practice in creating scattergrams, you can use the data in Figure 9.13 below to recreate the scattergram in Figure 9.14 on the next page by following the steps in this chapter.

```
▦ Untitled - SPSS Data Editor
File   Edit   View   Data   Transform   Analyze   Graphs   Utilities   Window   Help
```

21 : Absences

	School	Absences	var	var	var
1	8.00	4.00			
2	9.00	3.00			
3	10.00	3.00			
4	2.00	12.00			
5	5.00	13.00			
6	6.00	6.00			
7	6.00	7.00			
8	7.00	9.00			
9	6.00	8.00			
10	2.00	11.00			
11	1.00	8.00			
12	6.00	4.00			
13	9.00	.00			
14	4.00	5.00			
15	6.00	7.00			
16	6.00	6.00			
17	5.00	5.00			
18	6.00	6.00			
19	10.00	2.00			
20	.00	9.00			
21					
22					

Figure 9.13. Attitude Toward School Scores and Days Absent from School.

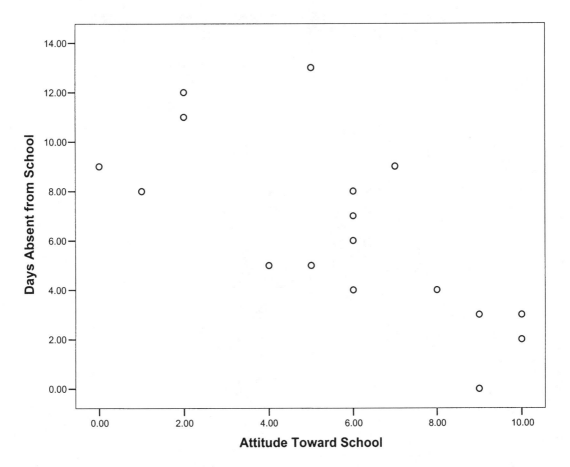

Figure 9.14. Scattergram for the relationship between Attitude Toward School and Days Absent from School (strong, inverse, linear relationship).

Strong Curvilinear Relationship

Two new sets of scores not previously shown in this book are presented in Figure 9.15 on the next page. The variables are Dosage (the dosage level of a prescription drug) and Improvement (improvement in patients' conditions). Figure 9.16 on the next page shows the scattergram for the relationship between the two sets of scores.

In the scattergram, the nature of the relationship is clear. For dosage levels 5 through 16, as the dosage level *goes up*, the improvement level *goes up*, suggesting a direct relationship. However, from dosage levels 18 through 28, the relationship changes direction such that as the dosage level *goes up* further, the improvement level *goes down*, suggesting an inverse relationship. In fact, the relationship is *neither* direct nor inverse. Instead, it is curvilinear (not capable of being described by a single straight line).

It is important to note that the correlational statistics presented in the next chapter are *not* appropriate for describing a curvilinear relationship, which will be illustrated in that chapter.

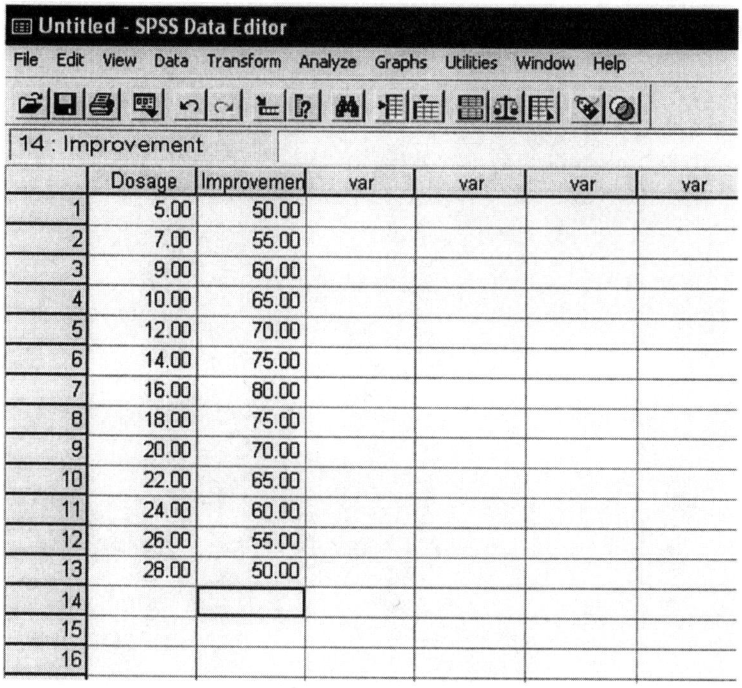

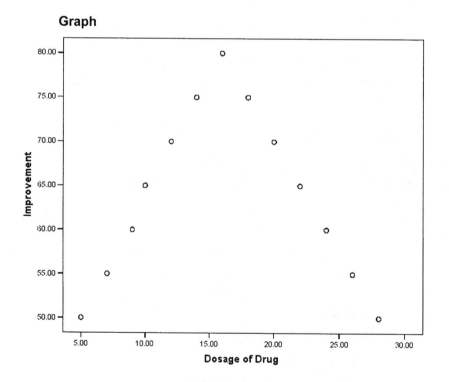

Figure 9.15. Dosage Level and Improvement.

Graph

Figure 9.16. Scattergram for the relationship between
Dosage Level and Improvement in Patients' Conditions
(strong, curvilinear relationship).

Formatting an SPSS Scattergram for Inclusion in a Research Report

Scattergrams should be given a figure number (in italics) followed by a caption (i.e., a descriptive title). Following the style of the American Psychological Association, the figure number and caption should be placed *below* the figure.[2] This is illustrated in Figures 9.15 and 9.16 on the previous page.

Describing a Scattergram in a Research Report

When a scattergram is presented in a research report, it should be briefly described in the text of the report. The description should also include the value of the corresponding correlation coefficient (whose symbol is r, which you will learn about in the next chapter). Example 9.1 below shows an example of such a description for the scattergram in Figure 9.10, which is the first scattergram in this chapter (see page 98).

Example 9.1

Statement that describes a relationship with a scattergram:

"The scattergram in Figure 9.10 indicates that there is a strong, linear, direct relationship between SAT Verbal scores and freshmen GPA ($r = .83$)."

Exercise for Chapter 9

1. Enter the scores shown in Table 9.1 below into SPSS. In the Variable View mode, name the first variable "Words" and label it "Words Per Minute Typed." (These are the words per minute typed on a typing test for applicants for jobs as office clerks.) Then, in the Data View mode, enter the scores in order (30, 44, 60, etc.).

Table 9.1

Number of Words Per Minute Typed on an Employment Test

30	44	60	65	50	55	53	44	35	31
44	53	61	40	52	53	50	33	52	45

---

[2] In APA style, table numbers and their captions (titles) are placed *above* tables, while figure numbers and their captions (titles) are placed *below* figures.

2. In the same data file as you entered the "Words Per Minute Typed," enter the scores shown in Table 9.2 below (for "Success on the Job") into SPSS. These are ratings of the employees' performances on the job after they were hired. The ratings were made by a supervisor on a scale from 1 (very poor) to 10 (excellent). First, in the Variable View mode, name this variable "Success" and label it "Success on the Job." Then, in the Data View mode, enter the scores in order (1, 3, 7, etc.).

Table 9.2

Success on the Job on a Scale from 0 to 10

1	3	7	9	8	4	3	4	2	4
5	6	9	4	6	5	8	4	7	5

3. Save the data file using the name "Words Typed and Success." (Click on "File," then "Save As," then name the file, and click "Save.") Note that you will be using this data file in the Exercise for Chapter 10.

4. Use SPSS to create a scattergram showing the relationship between the "Words Per Minute Typed" and "Success on the Job." When identifying the variables to be analyzed in SPSS, identify "Words Per Minute Typed" as the variable to be put on the X axis and "Success on the Job" as the variable to be put on the Y axis. If your instructor will be collecting your work, print out the scattergram.

   a. Is the relationship direct or inverse? _____

   b. Is the relationship perfect? _____

   c. Is the relationship strong? _____

   d. Is the relationship linear? _____

Chapter 10

Correlation Coefficients:
The Pearson *r* and Spearman's *rho*

***Learning objectives*:**
1. Define the term "correlation coefficient."
2. Identify when to use the Pearson *r*.
3. Identify when to use Spearman's *rho*.
4. Interpret a correlation coefficient in terms of its strength and direction.
5. Present a correlation coefficient in a research report.

Definition of "Correlation Coefficient"

A *correlation coefficient* is a statistic that indicates the strength and direction of the relationship between two variables for one group of participants. It provides a single numerical value to represent the relationship.

Correlation coefficients can range from –1.00 (perfect, inverse relationship) to 1.00 (perfect, direct relationship), with a value of 0.00 indicating no relationship. The meaning of *correlation coefficient* will be clearer after you examine the values of correlation coefficients shown later in this chapter for the scattergrams you saw in Chapter 9.

There are a number of different correlation coefficients. Two very frequently used ones (Pearson *r* and Spearman's *rho*) are discussed in this chapter.

When to Use the Pearson *r*

The Pearson *r* should be used when the following conditions are met:

a. You are interested in the relationship between two scale variables (i.e., interval or ratio variables). See Chapter 1 for more information on scale variables.
b. The distribution of scores is approximately symmetrical (i.e., not highly skewed). See Chapter 6 for more information on skewness. The most common type of symmetrical distribution is the normal distribution, which is not skewed.
c. The relationship is *not* curvilinear. This can be determined by examining a scattergram. (See the discussion of Figures 9.15 and 9.16 on pages 103 and 104 in Chapter 9 on page 104 for information identifying curvilinear relationships.) As you will see later in this chapter, if you compute a Pearson *r* for a curvilinear relationship, its value will be misleading.

if you compute a Pearson *r* for a curvilinear relationship, its value will be misleading.

When to Use Spearman's *rho*

Spearman's *rho* should be used when it is inappropriate to use the Pearson *r*. More specifically, it should be used when *either* of the following exists:

   a. One or both of the variables are ordinal (i.e., not at the scale level). See Chapter 1 for more information on ordinal variables.
   b. One or both of the distributions are clearly not symmetrical (i.e., highly skewed). See Chapter 6 for more information on skewness.

Like the Pearson *r*, Spearman's *rho* should *not* be computed to describe a curvilinear relationship.

Calculating the Pearson *r* and Spearman's *rho*

Step 1: Open the data file you saved with the file name "SAT and GPA" while working through Chapter 9.

If you cannot find the file, you will need to reenter the data by executing Steps 3 through 7 in Chapter 9. *Figure 10.1 below shows the data you entered in the saved file.*

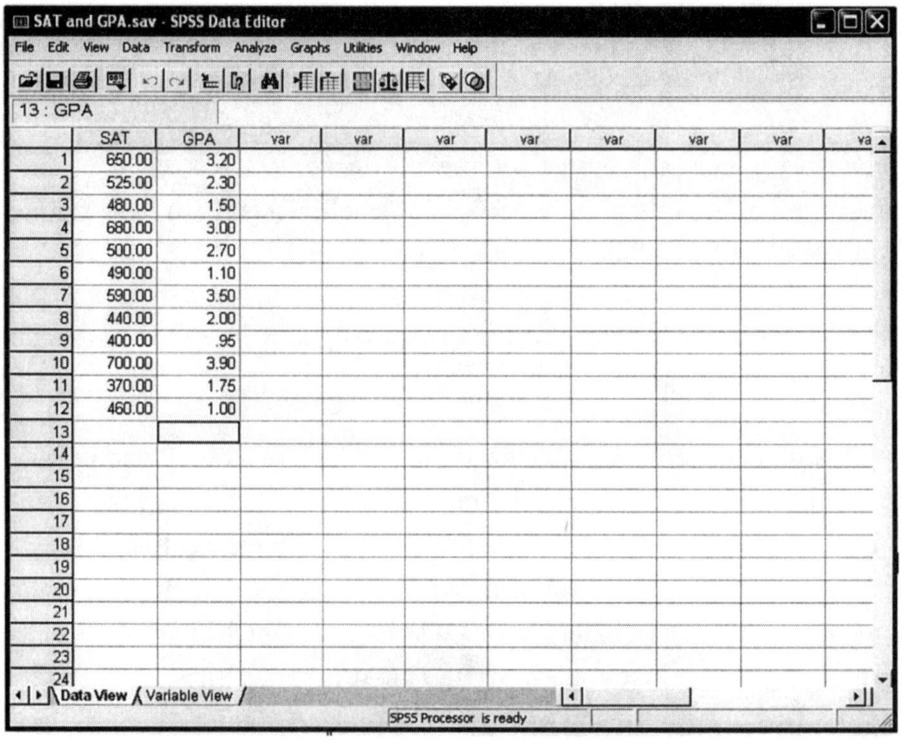

Figure 10.1. Data saved as "SAT and GPA" in Chapter 9 (see Figure 9.4 on page 93).

Step 2: Click on "Analyze," then move the cursor to "Correlate," then click on "Bivariate...."

See Figure 10.2 below. Note that the prefix "Bi-" in "Bivariate..." refers to "two," and the root "-variate" refers to "variable."

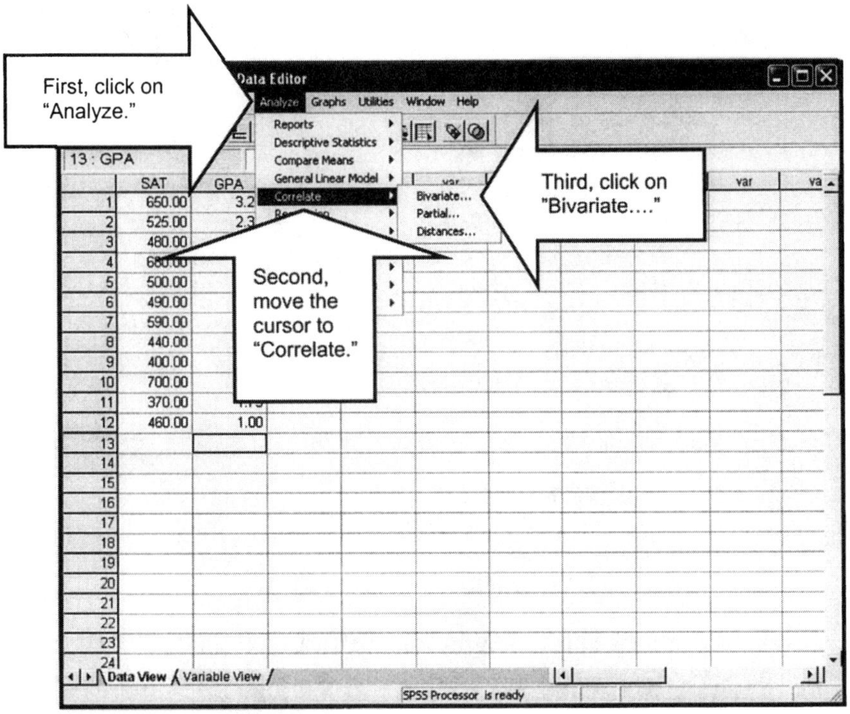

Figure 10.2. Sequence for Step 2.

Step 3: Click on the arrowhead to move "SAT Verbal Scores" to the "Variables" list.

Note that by default, SPSS selects the first variable in the list, which is highlighted in blue on your screen. In this case, SAT Verbal Scores is highlighted. Because this is one of the variables you want to include in the analysis, click on the arrowhead to move it to the "Variables" box on the right. *See Figure 10.3 on the next page.*

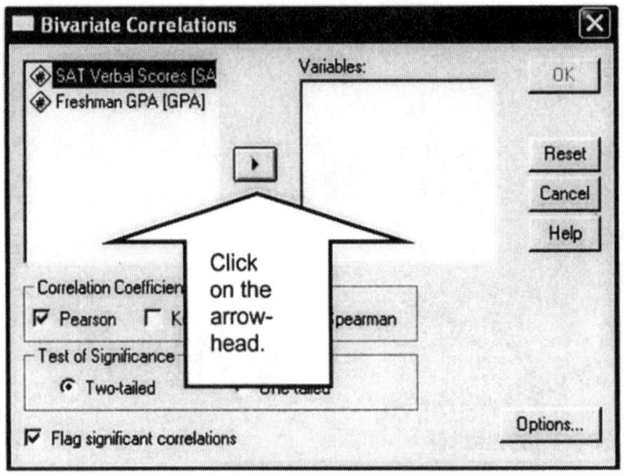

Figure 10.3. Step 3.

Step 4: Click on "Freshman GPA," and then click on the arrowhead again.

Figure 10.4 below shows what your screen should look like after executing Step 4. Notice that the names of both variables are now in the "Variables" box.

Step 5: Click on the small box to the left of "Spearman."

Note that by default, SPSS assumes you will want to calculate a Pearson *r*, so the box to the left of "Pearson" is already checked. By clicking to the left of "Spearman," you are instructing SPSS to also calculate Spearman's *rho*. A check mark will appear in the box after you click on it.

Step 6: Click OK.

See Figure 10.4 below.

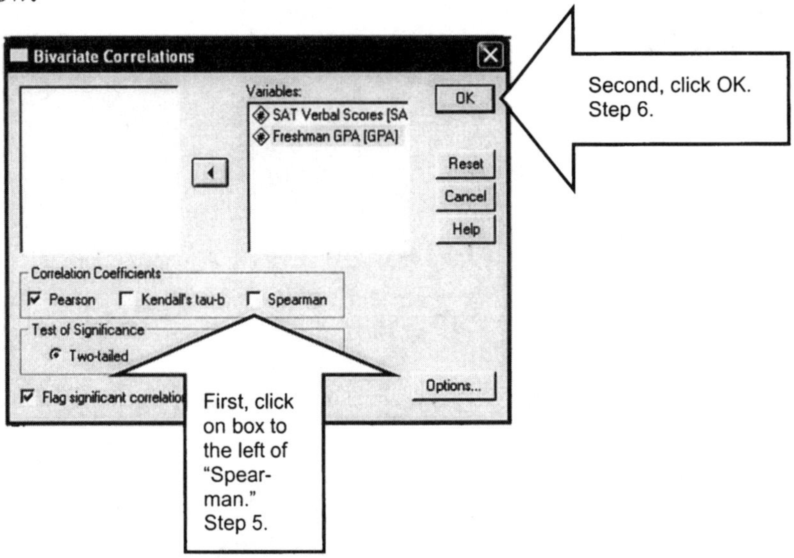

Figure 10.4. Steps 5 and 6.

After executing Step 6, the SPSS output shown in Figure 10.5 below will appear on your screen.

Correlations

Correlations

		SAT Verbal Scores	Freshman GPA
SAT Verbal Scores	Pearson Correlation	1	.831**
	Sig. (2-tailed)		.001
	N	12	12
Freshman GPA	Pearson Correlation	.831**	1
	Sig. (2-tailed)	.001	
	N	12	12

**. Correlation is significant at the 0.01 level (2-tailed).

Notice that the Pearson *r* = .831.

➜ Nonparametric Correlations

Correlations

			SAT Verbal Scores	Freshman GPA
Spearman's rho	SAT Verbal Scores	Correlation Coefficient	1.000	.825**
		Sig. (2-tailed)	.	.001
		N	12	12
	Freshman GPA	Correlation Coefficient	.825**	1.000
		Sig. (2-tailed)	.001	.
		N	12	12

**. Correlation is significant at the 0.01 level (2-tailed).

Notice that Spearman's *rho* = .825.

Figure 10.5. Output produced after Step 6.

Interpreting the SPSS Output

As you can see in Figure 10.5 above, the value of the Pearson *r* is .831. Because it is a positive number, the relationship is direct. See Chapter 9 for examples of direct and inverse relationships illustrated with scattergrams.

Direct relationships can range in value from 0.00 (no relationship) to 1.00 (perfect relationship). Since .831 is close to 1.00, .831 can be called *very strong* (see Information Box 10.1 on the next page).

For the same data, the value of Spearman's *rho* (.825) is similar to the value of the Pearson *r*. As a general rule, when the conditions for using the Pearson *r* discussed near the beginning of this chapter are met (as they are with the distributions of SAT and GPA), the two correlation coefficients will be similar in value.

Information Box 10.1

Describing the Strength of Relationships Based on Correlation Coefficients

There are no universal rules for describing in words the strength of relationships indicated by correlation coefficients. Therefore, the following should be regarded only as *rough rules of thumb*.

A value of 0.00 indicates "no relationship."

Values between .01 and .24 may be called "weak."

Values between .25 and .49 may be called "moderate."

Values between .50 and .74 may be called "moderately strong."

Values between .75 and .99 may be called "very strong."

A value of 1.00 is called "perfect."

For describing the strength of relationships with correlation coefficients, what is true in the positive is true in the negative. Thus, for instance, values between $-.75$ and $-.99$ (like values of .75 and .99) would also be called "very strong," even though they represent inverse relationships.

Reporting Correlation Coefficients in a Research Report

When the conditions for using the Pearson *r* discussed near the beginning of this chapter are met, the Pearson *r* is the correlation coefficient that should be reported and interpreted. A Pearson *r* can be reported in a sentence as illustrated in Example 10.1 below. Note that the statement should indicate the direction of the relationship (i.e., direct *or* inverse) and the strength (e.g., *very* strong). Also, note that the symbol "*r*" should be italicized. Finally, note that it is typical to round correlation coefficients to two decimal places before reporting them.

Example 10.1

Statement that presents a Pearson *r*.

"The relationship between SAT Verbal scores and freshman GPA is direct and very strong (Pearson *r* = .83)."

Example 10.2 below shows how the Pearson *r* could be reported.

Example 10.2

"The value of the Pearson *r* is 1.00, which indicates a *perfect, direct relationship*."

For additional practice, you can analyze the scores by executing the steps in this chapter to confirm its value.

Information Box 10.2

Variations on the Names for the Pearson r and Spearman's rho in Research Reports

The full, formal name of the Pearson *r* is "Pearson product-moment correlation coefficient," a term that sometimes is used by researchers in their research reports. Variations on terms for the Pearson *r* that can be found in published research reports are:

- Pearson correlation coefficient, and
- product-moment correlation coefficient.

If a researcher uses just the term "correlation coefficient," he or she is probably referring to the Pearson *r*. Use of only this term is *not* recommended because it does not indicate which type of correlation coefficient is being reported.

The full, formal name of Spearman's *rho* is "Spearman's rank-order correlation coefficient." Variations on terms for Spearman's *rho* that can be found in published research reports are:

- rank-order correlation coefficient, and
- *rho* (without Spearman's name).

Exercise for Chapter 10

1. Open the data file you saved with the name "Words Typed and Success" in the exercise for Chapter 9. (If you cannot find the data file, you will need to reenter the scores shown in that exercise.) Calculate the values of the Pearson *r* and Spearman's *rho*. Note that the data in this file meet the criteria for using the Pearson *r*.

   a. What is the value of the Pearson *r*? _____

   b. What is the value of Spearman's *rho*? _____

   c. Write a sentence that presents the Pearson *r* for the relationship between words typed and success:

   _____

   _____

Notes:

Chapter 11

The *t* Test for a Single Sample Mean

***Learning objectives*:**

1. Identify purpose of the *t* test for a single sample mean.
2. Conduct a *t* test to determine the significance of the difference between a single sample mean and a test value (i.e., a known value or hypothetical value).
3. Interpret the results of the *t* test in terms of the null hypothesis and statistical significance.
4. Present the results of the *t* test in a research report.

Purpose of the *t* Test for a Single Sample Mean

The purpose of the *t* test for a single sample mean is to determine whether the mean for a random sample of participants differs significantly from a known value or a hypothetical value. Example 11.1 below illustrates the need to test a sample mean against a known population mean.

Example 11.1
A sample mean to be compared with a known value.

A researcher knows that the national average on the ABC Attitude Toward Math Scale is 4.0. The researcher draws a random sample of students from an urban school district, administers the attitude scale to the sample, and obtains a mean of 3.7. To determine if the sample mean of 3.7 is significantly different from the national average of 4.0, the researcher needs to conduct a *t* test for a single sample.[1]

When to Use the *t* Test for a Single Sample Mean

The *t* test for a sample mean is used when the mean for one set of scores is to be compared with a known or hypothetical mean. As you know from earlier chapters, the mean should be computed only for *interval* or *ratio* data (known as *scale* data in SPSS), and only for distributions that are not highly skewed.

---

[1] In this example, the "known value" is the national mean. The *t* test can also be used to test a sample mean against a "hypothetical value" such as a value derived from theory. In SPSS, the "known value" or "hypothetical value" is known as the "Test Value."

Conducting a *t* Test for a Single Sample Mean

Step 1: Open the data file you saved with the file name "Attitude Toward Math" when completing the exercise for Chapter 2.

If you cannot find the saved data file, you will need to reenter the data, which are shown in *Figure 11.1 below.*

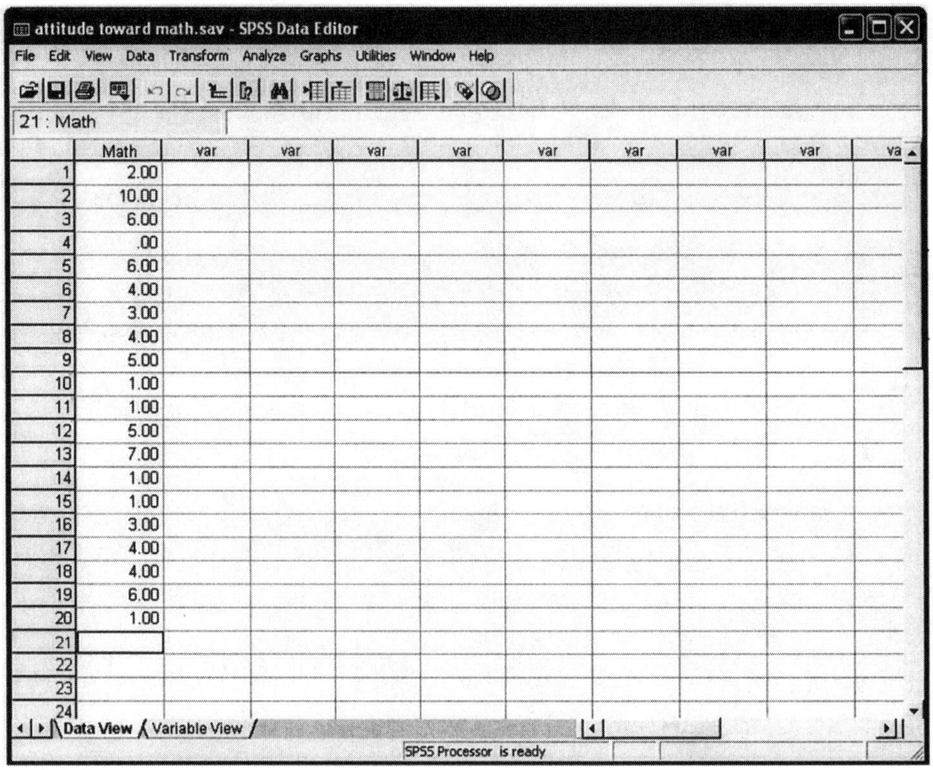

Figure 11.1. Data for Attitude Toward Math from the Exercise for Chapter 2.

Step 2: Click on "Analyze," then move the cursor to "Compare Means," and then click on "One-Sample T Test...."

See Figure 11.2 on the next page.

Figure 11.2. Sequence for Step 2.

After executing Step 2, the "One-Sample T Test..." dialog box will appear on the screen.

Step 3: Click on the arrowhead to move the variable from the box on the left to the "Test Variable(s)" box.

See Figure 11.3 below.

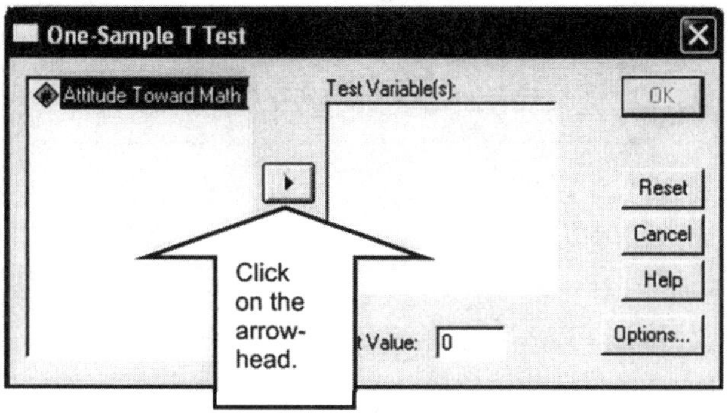

Figure 11.3. Step 3.

Step 4: Type the number "4.0" in the "Test Value" box.

Note that you are entering the national average of 4.0 as the value to test against. The value of 4.0 comes from Example 11.1 on page 115.

See the arrow for Step 4 in Figure 11.4 below.

Step 5: Click OK.

See the arrow for Step 5 in Figure 11.4 below.

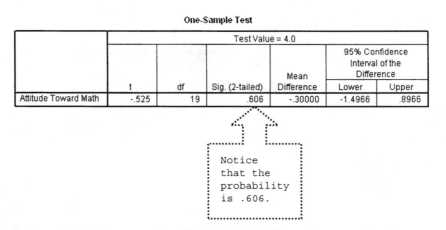

Figure 11.4. Steps 4 and 5.

After executing Step 5, the output shown in ***Figure 11.5 below*** will appear.

→ T-Test

One-Sample Statistics

	N	Mean	Std. Deviation	Std. Error Mean
Attitude Toward Math	20	3.7000	2.55672	.57170

One-Sample Test

	Test Value = 4.0					
					95% Confidence Interval of the Difference	
	t	df	Sig. (2-tailed)	Mean Difference	Lower	Upper
Attitude Toward Math	-.525	19	.606	-.30000	-1.4966	.8966

Notice that the probability is .606.

Figure 11.5. Output after Step 5, including the *t* test for one sample.

Interpreting the SPSS Output

In the output in ***Figure 11.5 on the previous page***, the mean for the sample is 3.7000, and the value of *t* is –.525. The probability that the null hypothesis is true is .606 [indicated in SPSS with the term "Sig. (2-tailed)"]. Note that by default, SPSS uses a two-tailed test, which is by far the most frequently used. To interpret the probability value of .606, use the following guidelines, which are repeated in Appendix A for reference in future chapters. See Appendix A for examples.

a.   If the probability displayed by SPSS is equal to or less than .001, declare the difference to be statistically significant at the .001 level.

b.   If the probability displayed by SPSS is equal to or less than .01 (but greater than .001), declare the difference to be statistically significant at the .01 level.

c.   If the probability displayed by SPSS is equal to or less than .05 (but greater than .01), declare the difference to be statistically significant at the .05 level.

d.   If the probability displayed by SPSS is *greater* than .05, declare the difference to be *not* statistically significant (i.e., *in*significant) at the .05 level.

Because .606 (in the output in Figure 11.5 on the previous page) is greater than .05, the difference is *not* statistically significant. Because it is *not* statistically significant, the null hypothesis should *not* be rejected.

Describing the Results of a *t* Test for a Single Sample Mean in a Research Report
Describing the Results of an Insignificant *t* Test

First, report the mean and standard deviation for the sample (in this case, the district sample) as well as the known value (in this case, the national population value). Then, report the value of *t*, and indicate whether it is statistically significant. This is illustrated in Example 11.2 below for the output in Figure 11.5 on the previous page.

Example 11.2
Statement that presents the results of an insignificant *t* test for the output in Figure 11.5 on the previous page.

"For the local district sample, the values of the mean and standard deviation are 3.70 and 2.56, respectively. The national mean is 4.00. The difference between the sample mean and the national mean is not statistically significant at the .05 level ($t = -.525$, $df = 19$)."

It is important to note that SPSS uses the letters "T" and "t." However, in research reports, you should use a lowercase, italicized *t*, which is done in Example 11.2 above. Also, note that in various places, SPSS hyphenates "T-Test." In the social and behavioral sciences, this term is *not* hyphenated. Thus, when discussing the analysis in a research report, it is more appropriate to state "A *t* test was used…" than to state "A T-Test was used.…"

Describing the Results of a Significant *t* Test

As with an insignificant *t* test (see the discussion immediately above), for a significant test, report the mean and standard deviation for the sample (in this case, the district sample) as well as the known value, followed by the results of the *t* test. Suppose, for instance, that the statewide mean on the Attitude Toward Math scale is 2.50. As you know from Example 11.2 on the previous page, the district mean is 3.70. Following Steps 1 through 5 and using 2.50 as the "Test Value," the output in Figure 11.6 below would be obtained. Note that the probability, indicated by "Sig. (2-tailed)" in the output, is .049, which is less than .05, indicating that the difference is statistically significant. Example 11.3 below illustrates how the output in Figure 11.6 below could be reported.

➔ **T-Test**

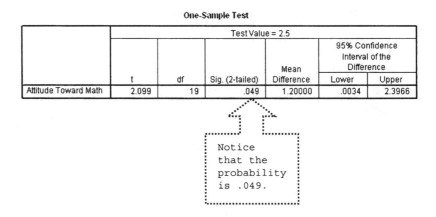

One-Sample Statistics

	N	Mean	Std. Deviation	Std. Error Mean
Attitude Toward Math	20	3.7000	2.55672	.57170

One-Sample Test

	Test Value = 2.5					
					95% Confidence Interval of the Difference	
	t	df	Sig. (2-tailed)	Mean Difference	Lower	Upper
Attitude Toward Math	2.099	19	.049	1.20000	.0034	2.3966

Notice that the probability is .049.

Figure 11.6. Output with a test value of 2.50.

Example 11.3
Statement that presents the results of a significant *t* test for the output in Figure 11.6 above.

"For the local district sample, the values of the mean and standard deviation are 3.70 and 2.56, respectively. The statewide mean is 2.50. The difference between the sample mean and the statewide mean is statistically significant at the .05 level (*t* = 2.099, *df* = 19)."

Information Box 11.1

Interpreting Negative and Positive Values of t

> For the *t* test for a sample mean, a negative value of *t* indicates that the sample mean is lower than the "Test Value," while a positive value of *t* indicates that the sample value is higher than the "Test Value." The sign (negative or positive) has no other implications.

Information Box 11.2

Reporting on the Null Hypothesis in Research Reports

> In research reports published in academic journals, the null hypothesis is very rarely explicitly mentioned. Instead, researchers usually report only whether a difference is statistically significant or not. Readers of the reports are assumed to know that if a difference is significant, the null hypothesis has been rejected.
>
> In term papers, theses, and dissertations, it is sometimes desirable to mention the decision made about the null hypothesis in order to illustrate that the writer understands the purpose of a significance test. Under this circumstance, it would be appropriate to add this sentence at the end of Example 11.2 on page 119: "Thus, the null hypothesis was not rejected." At the end of Example 11.3 on page 120, this sentence could be added: "Thus, the null hypothesis was rejected."

Exercise for Chapter 11

1. The scores shown below are the number-correct scores on a standardized reading test for a random sample of sixth-grade students from the Washington Elementary School. The mean for the school district (the "Test Value") is: $M = 32.00$. Conduct a *t* test to determine whether the known value of 32.00 for the district is significantly different from the mean score for Washington Elementary School. Note that 32.00 is the "Test Value" in SPSS. Then, answer the questions that follow.

   Scores for a random sample at Washington Elementary School:

   27, 28, 29, 30, 31, 32, 33, 34, 35, 36, 38, 40

   a. What is the value of the mean for the sample at Washington Elementary School? _____

   b. What is the value of *t*? _____

c. What is the associated probability? _____

d. Is the difference between the district mean of 32.00 and the mean at Washington Elementary School statistically significant at the .05 level? _____

e. Write a statement of the results of the significance test.

_____

_____

Chapter 12

Paired-Samples *t* Test

> **Learning objectives:**
> 1. Identify the purpose of the paired-samples *t* test.
> 2. Conduct a *t* test to determine the significance of the difference between the means of two paired samples (i.e., dependent means).
> 3. Interpret the results of a *t* test in terms of the null hypothesis and statistical significance.
> 4. Present the results of the *t* test in a research report.

Purpose of the Paired-Samples *t* Test

As you know from Chapter 11, the *t* test can be used to determine the statistical significance of the difference between two means. In Chapter 11, the procedure for testing the difference between a known mean (such as a population mean) with a sample mean was covered.

In this chapter, you will learn how to conduct the *paired-samples t test*.[1] This test is appropriate when each score underlying one mean has been paired (i.e., matched) with a score underlying the other mean. Example 12.1 below illustrates the meaning of *paired samples* (i.e., with paired scores).

Example 12.1
An experiment with paired scores.

A researcher drew a random sample from a population and administered a depression scale to the sample. This administration of the scale yielded *pretest scores*, for which the researcher computed a mean. Then, the researcher administered a new antidepressant drug to the sample. Next, the researcher administered the depression scale again, which yielded *posttest scores*. As a result, for each pretest score earned by an individual, there is an associated posttest score for the same individual. These sets of scores are *paired scores*.[2]

To conduct the paired-samples *t* test, you will be analyzing the scores in Table 12.1 on the next page, which are based on Example 12.1 above. The researcher wants to determine if the difference between the mean of the pretest scores is significantly different from the mean of the

---

[1] In statistics textbooks, the *paired-samples t* test is often called the "*t* test for dependent means."
[2] Compare this example with Example 13.1 on page 133 in Chapter 13, which illustrates *independent samples*, for which there is no pairing of scores underlying the two means.

posttest scores. Note that each pretest score is *paired* with a posttest score (i.e., the pretest score of 10 for Participant Number 1 is paired with his or her posttest score of 9 by being placed on the same row).

Table 12.1
Pretest and Posttest Depression Scores

Participant number	Pretest score	Posttest score
1	10	9
2	12	9
3	9	10
4	15	15
5	11	8
6	14	10
7	8	9
8	13	10
9	12	7

Conducting a Paired-Samples *t* Test

Step 1: In the Variable View mode, name the first variable "Pre" and label it "Pretest." Name the second variable "Post" and label it "Posttest."

First, click on the Variable View tab to make sure you are in the Variable View mode. Then, name and label the variables. ***See Figure 12.1 below.***

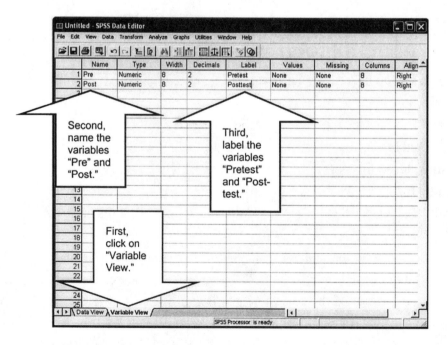

Figure 12.1. Sequence for Step 1.

Step 2: Click on the Data View tab.

See Figure 12.2 below.

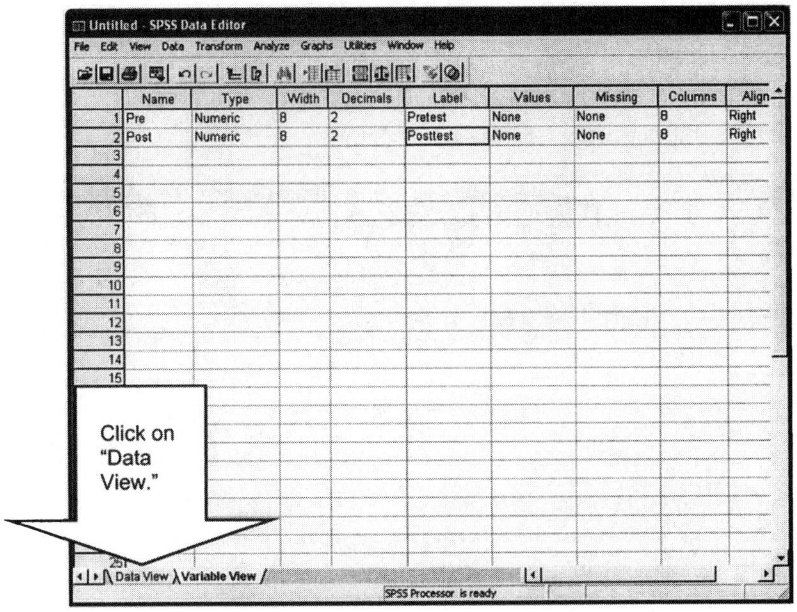

Figure 12.2. Step 2.

Step 3: Enter the pretest and posttest scores.

See the scores entered for Step 3 in Figure 12.3 below.

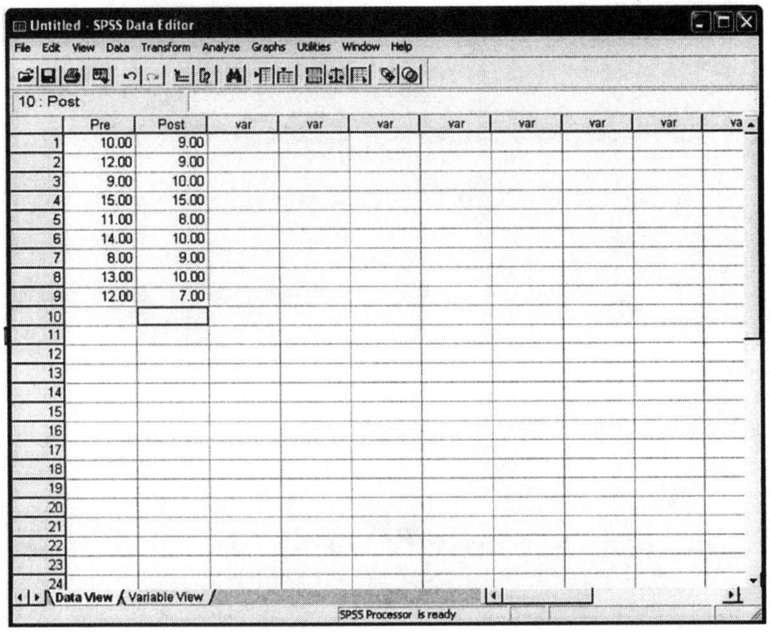

Figure 12.3. Step 3.

Step 4: Click on "Analyze," move the cursor to "Compare Means," and click on "Paired-Samples T Test...."

See Figure 12.4 below.

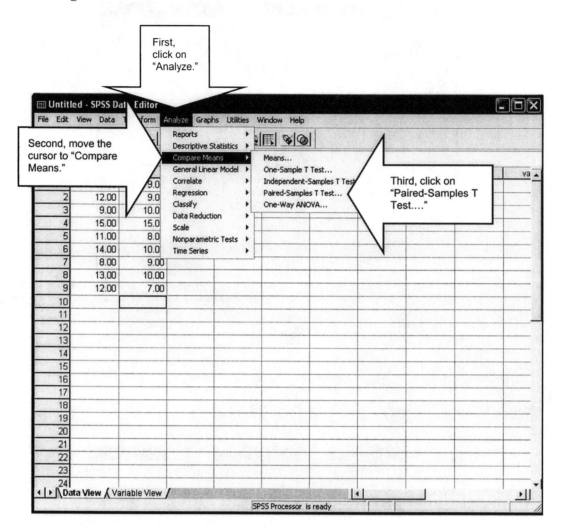

Figure 12.4. Sequence for Step 4.

After executing Step 4, the "Paired-Samples T Test..." dialog box will appear on the screen.

Step 5: Click on "Pretest," then click on "Posttest," and then click on the arrow-head.

See the arrows for Step 5 in Figure 12.5 on the next page.

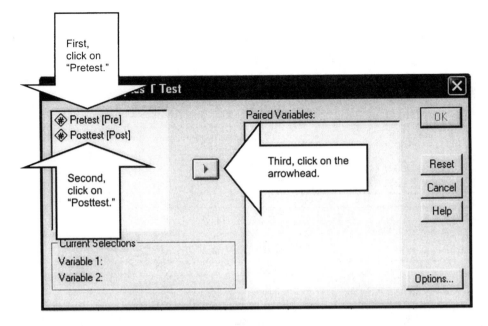

Figure 12.5. Sequence for Step 5.

Step 6: Click OK.

See Figure 12.6 below.

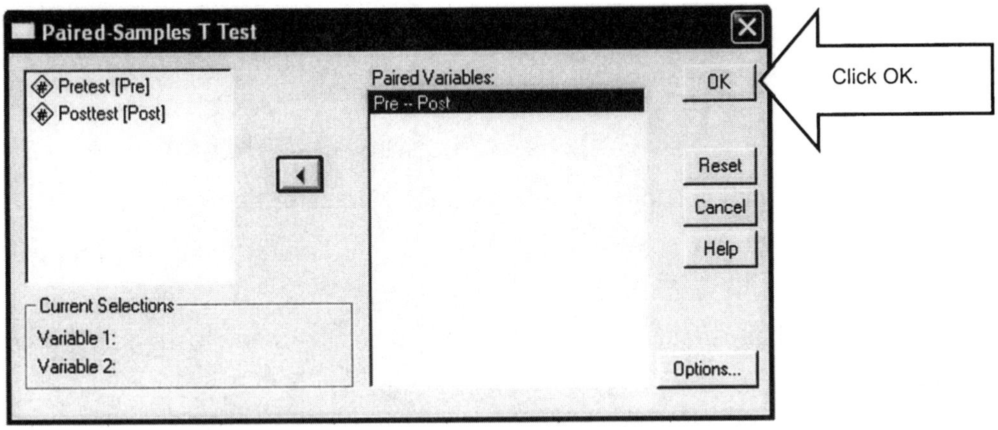

Figure 12.6. Step 6.

After executing Step 6, you will see the output in Figure 12.7 on the next page.

→ T-Test

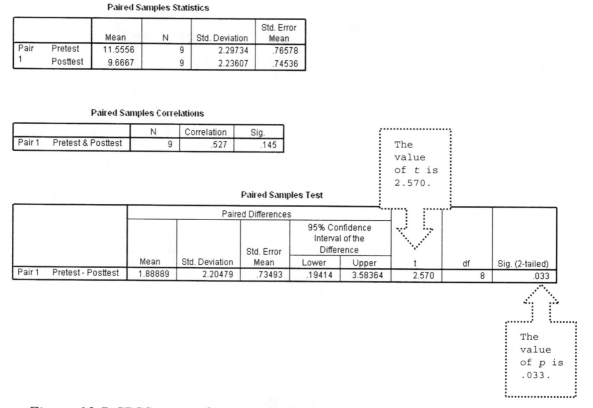

Paired Samples Statistics

		Mean	N	Std. Deviation	Std. Error Mean
Pair 1	Pretest	11.5556	9	2.29734	.76578
	Posttest	9.6667	9	2.23607	.74536

Paired Samples Correlations

		N	Correlation	Sig.
Pair 1	Pretest & Posttest	9	.527	.145

The value of *t* is 2.570.

Paired Samples Test

		Paired Differences					t	df	Sig. (2-tailed)
		Mean	Std. Deviation	Std. Error Mean	95% Confidence Interval of the Difference				
					Lower	Upper			
Pair 1	Pretest - Posttest	1.88889	2.20479	.73493	.19414	3.58364	2.570	8	.033

The value of *p* is .033.

Figure 12.7. SPSS output for the paired-samples *t* test.

Interpreting the SPSS Output

In the output in Figure 12.7 above, note that SPSS refers to the probability of .033 as "Sig. (2-tailed)." Because .033 is less than .05 (but greater than .01), the difference between the means is statistically significant at the .05 level. (Refer to the decision rules in Appendix A for interpreting probability levels.) When the difference is statistically significant, the *null hypothesis* is rejected.

Describing the Results of a *t* Test for Paired Samples in a Research Report
Reporting the Results of a Significant *t* Test

First, report the mean and standard deviation for each set of scores. Then, report the value of *t*, and indicate whether it is statistically significant. This is illustrated in Example 12.2 on the next page for the output in Figure 12.7 above.

Example 12.2
Statement that presents the results of a significant *t* test for the output in Figure 12.7 on the previous page.

"The mean depression score decreased from 11.56 (*sd* = 2.30) on the pretest to 9.67 (*sd* = 2.24) on the posttest. The difference between the two means is statistically significant at the .05 level (*t* = 2.57, *df* = 8)."

As mentioned in the previous chapter, it is important to note that SPSS uses the letters "T" and "t." However, in research reports, you should use a lowercase, italicized *t*, which is done in Example 12.2 above. Also, note that in various places, SPSS hyphenates "T-Test." In the social and behavioral sciences, this term is *not* hyphenated. Thus, when discussing the analysis in a research report, it is more appropriate to state "A *t* test was used…" than to state "A T-Test was used.…"

Reporting the Results of an Insignificant *t* Test

Report the means and standard deviations for the two sets of scores, followed by the results of the *t* test. Figure 12.8 below shows the results of an insignificant *t* test for differences in algebra scores from pretest to posttest. (The scores on which the *t* test was conducted are not shown in this book. The results of the *t* test on them are given in order to illustrate how to report the results of an insignificant *t* test.)

Note that the probability of .447 is greater than .05, so the difference is not statistically significant. Also, note that the fact that the value of *t* is negative has no bearing on significance; significance is determined solely by the probability (the value of *p*).

➜ **T-Test**

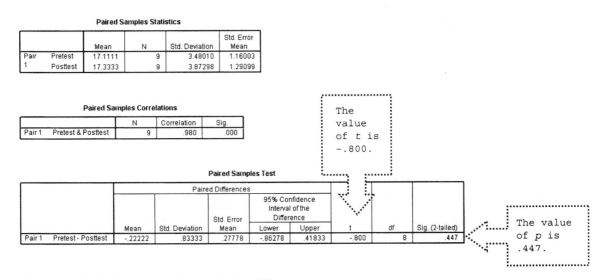

Figure 12.8. Output with an insignificant *t* test.

For the insignificant *t* test in Figure 12.8 on the previous page, a statement reporting the results is presented in Example 12.3 below.

Example 12.3
Statement that presents the results of an insignificant *t* test for the output in Figure 12.8 on the previous page.

"The average algebra score increased only slightly from 17.11 (*sd* = 3.48) on the pretest to 17.33 (*sd* = 3.87) on the posttest. The difference between the two means is not statistically significant at the .05 level (*t* = −.800, *df* = 8)."

Exercise for Chapter 12

Analyze the data in Table 12.2 below, which contains changes in self-esteem scores from pretest (before psychological counseling) to posttest (after psychological counseling). Follow the steps in this chapter to conduct a paired-samples *t* test, and then answer the questions that follow.

Table 12.2

Pretest and Posttest Self-Esteem Scores Before and After Psychological Counseling

Participant number	Pretest score	Posttest score
1	30	28
2	33	29
3	29	30
4	27	31
5	26	29
6	37	37
7	40	41
8	35	40
9	36	37
10	35	38

a. What is the value of the mean for the pretest? _____

b. What is the mean for the posttest? _____

c. What is the value of *t*? _____

d. What is the associated probability? _____

e. Is the difference between the pretest and posttest means statistically significant at the .05 level? _____

f. Write a statement of the results of the significance test.

_____

_____

Notes:

Chapter 13

Independent-Samples *t* Test

Learning objectives:

1. Identify the purpose of the independent-samples *t* test.
2. Conduct a *t* test to determine the significance of the difference between the means of two independent samples.
3. Interpret the results of a *t* test in terms of the null hypothesis and statistical significance.
4. Present the results of the *t* test in a research report.

Purpose of the Independent-Samples *t* Test

As you know from Chapters 11 and 12, the *t* test can be used to determine the statistical significance of the difference between two means. In Chapter 11, the procedure for testing the difference between a known mean (such as a population mean) and a sample mean was covered. In Chapter 12, the use of the *t* test for paired samples was covered. In this chapter, you will learn how to conduct a *t* test for *two samples* that are *independent* of each other. The term *independent* indicates that there is no relationship (no matching or pairing) of scores from one sample to the other. Example 13.1 below has *independent samples*.[1]

Example 13.1
An experiment with two independent samples.

A researcher drew a random sample from a population and showed the sample a film on the consequences of driving while intoxicated. This sample was the experimental group. For a control group, the researcher independently drew a separate random sample from the same population to which the film was *not* shown. Then, a questionnaire on attitudes toward drinking and driving was administered, and the mean for each sample was computed. Because selection of the individuals for the experimental group had no bearing on the selection of individuals for the control group, the two samples are said to be *independent*. In other words, they were separately and independently drawn from a population.[2]

---

[1] In statistics textbooks, the *t* test for independent samples is often called the "*t* test for independent means."

[2] Contrast Example 13.1 with Example 12.1 on page 123 in Chapter 12, which has dependent samples (i.e., paired samples).

Assigning Numerical Codes to Identify Groups

You will be entering the data in Table 13.1 below into SPSS, which are based on Example 13.1 on the previous page. Note that there are two variables in the table. The first variable is "Group" (experimental or control). For analysis by SPSS, you will use the following codes, as shown in the table: 1 = experimental group and 2 = control group.

The second variable is "attitudes toward drinking and driving." See Example 13.1 on the previous page for a description of the design of the experiment. Note that *higher scores* indicate a *more positive* attitude toward drinking and driving.

Table 13.1

Attitudes Toward Drinking and Driving for Experimental and Control Groups

Participant number	Group	Codes for groups	Attitudes toward drinking and driving
1	Experimental	1	12
2	Control	2	14
3	Control	2	14
4	Experimental	1	10
5	Experimental	1	12
6	Control	2	15
7	Experimental	1	8
8	Control	2	16
9	Experimental	1	12
10	Control	2	10
11	Experimental	1	9
12	Control	1	11

Conducting an Independent-Samples *t* Test

Step 1: Click on "Variable View," name the first variable "Group," and label it "Experimental and Control Groups."

See the arrows for Step 1 in Figure 13.1 on the next page.

Step 2: Click on "Values."

See the arrow for Step 2 in Figure 13.1 on the next page.

Step 3: Click on the small gray box that will appear under "Values" after executing Step 2.

See the arrow for Step 3 in Figure 13.1 on the next page.

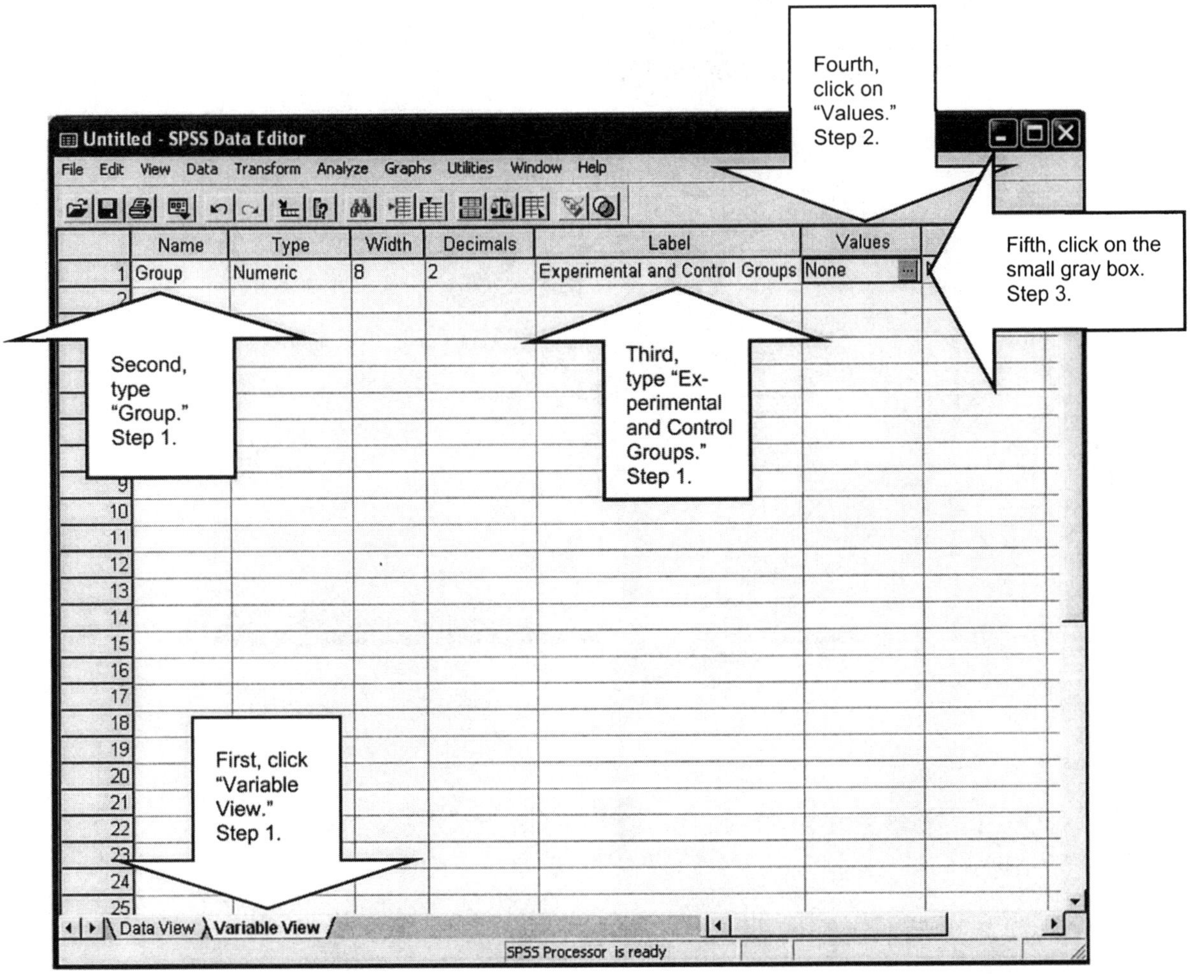

Figure 13.1. Steps 1, 2, and 3.

After executing Step 3, the "Value Labels" dialog box will appear on the screen.

Step 4: Type the number "1" in the space to the right of the word "Value" in the dialog box.

See the arrow for Step 4 in Figure 13.2 on the next page.

Step 5: Type the words "Experimental Group" in the space to the right of the words "Value Label."

By executing Steps 4 and 5, you are indicating that the number 1 is the code (i.e., called the "value label" in SPSS) for the experimental group. Do ***not*** type the quotation marks; SPSS will automatically add them after Step 6. ***See the arrow for Step 5 in Figure 13.2 on the next page.***

Step 6: Click "Add."

See the arrow for Step 6 in Figure 13.2 below.

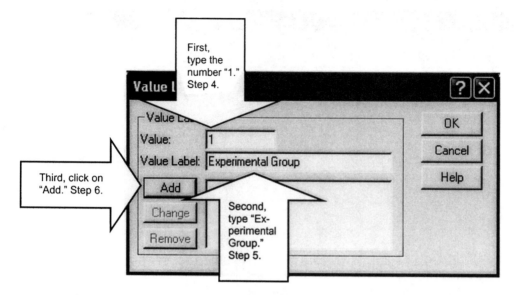

Figure 13.2. Steps 4, 5, and 6.

Step 7: Repeat Steps 4 though 6, using the Value of "2" and the Value Label "Control Group."

Be sure to click "Add" at the end of Step 6.

Step 8: Click OK.

See Figure 13.3 below.

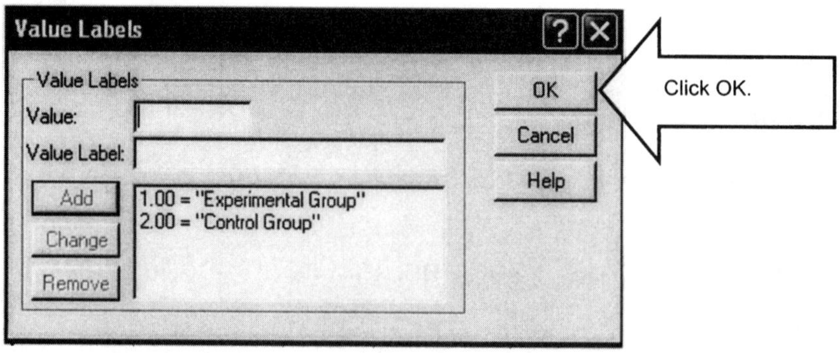

Figure 13.3. Step 8.

Step 9: Name the second variable "Attitudes," and label it "Attitudes Toward Drinking and Driving."

See Figure 13.4 below.

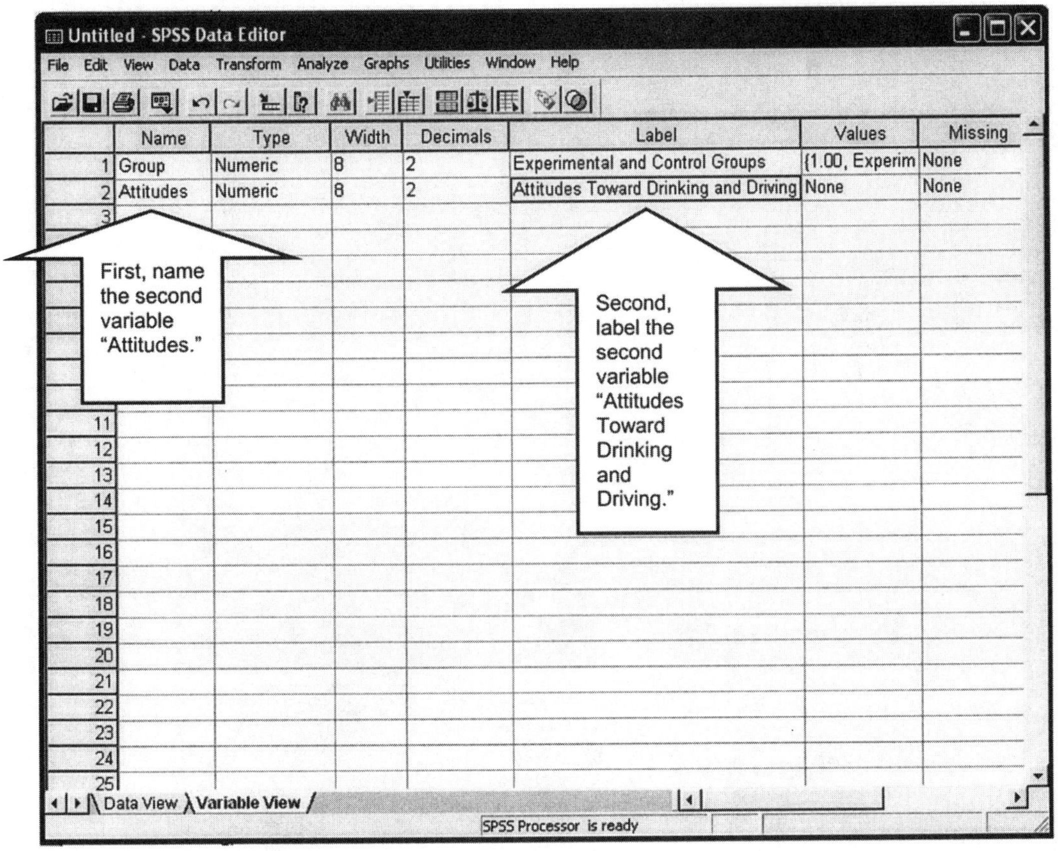

Figure 13.4. Sequence for Step 9.

Step 10: Click on the "Data View" tab, and enter the codes and scores from Table 13.1 on page 134 for the two variables.

For the variable named "Group," use the codes 1 and 2 (*not* the words experimental group and control group). ***Figure 13.5 on the next page*** shows the Data View screen after the scores for the two variables have been entered. Remember to press the Enter or down-arrow key after entering the last score for attitudes (the score of 11).

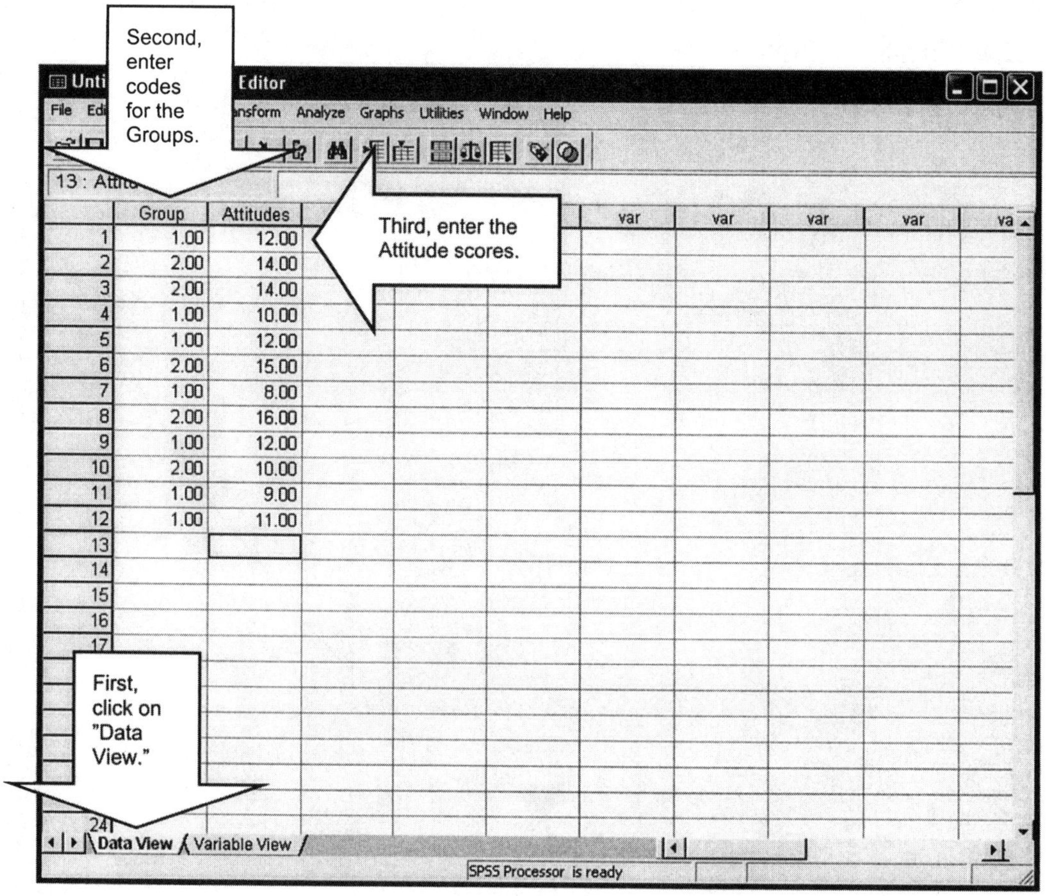

Figure 13.5. Sequence for Step 10.

Step 11: Click on "Analyze," then put the cursor on "Compare Means," and then click "Independent-Samples T Test...."

See Figure 13.6 on the next page.

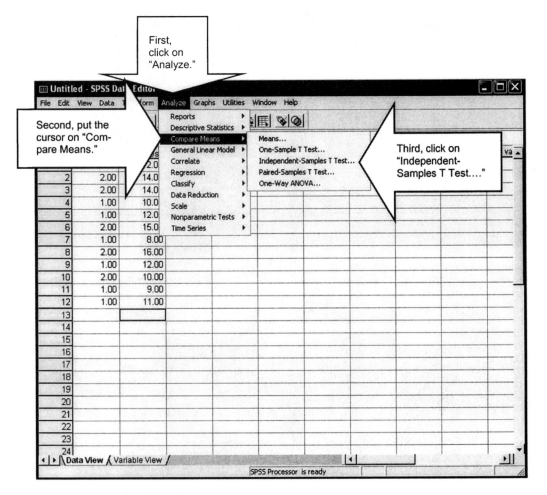

Figure 13.6. Sequence for Step 11.

After executing Step 11, the "Independent-Samples T Test…" dialog box will appear. In it, the variable labeled "Experimental and Control Groups" will already be selected as indicated by being highlighted in blue.

Step 12: Click on the bottom arrowhead to move "Experimental and Control Groups" to the "Grouping Variable" box, and then click on "Define Groups."

Executing this step will identify "Experimental and Control Groups" as the independent variable.

See Figure 13.7 on the next page.

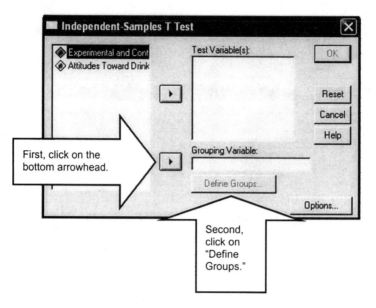

Figure 13.7. Step 12.

After executing Step 12, the "Define Groups" dialog box will appear on the screen.

Step 13: In the "Define Groups" dialog box, type in "1" for Group 1 and "2" for Group 2, and then click "Continue."

See Figure 13.8 below.

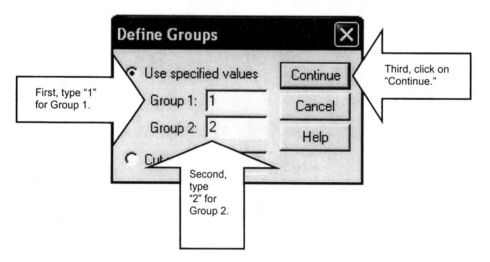

Figure 13.8. Sequence for Step 13.

Step 14: Click on "Attitudes Toward Drinking and Driving" to highlight it, and then click the top arrowhead to move it to the "Test Variable(s)" box.

See Figure 13.9 below.

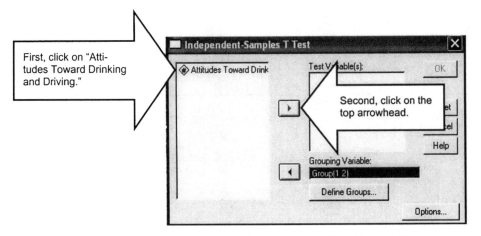

Figure 13.9. Sequence for Step 14.

Information Box 13.1

Dependent Variable and Test Variable in SPSS

In an experiment in which treatments are given to participants, the outcome variable (such as attitudes toward drinking and driving) is referred to as the *dependent variable*. In contrast, in SPSS, the dependent variable is called the *test variable*. (See Step 14.)

Step 15: Click OK.

See Figure 13.10 below.

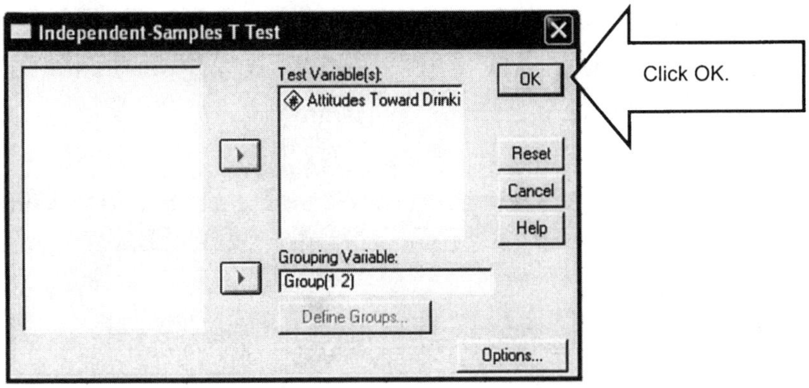

Figure 13.10. Step 15.

After executing Step 15, the raw SPSS output shown in Figure 13.11 below will appear.

➔ T-Test

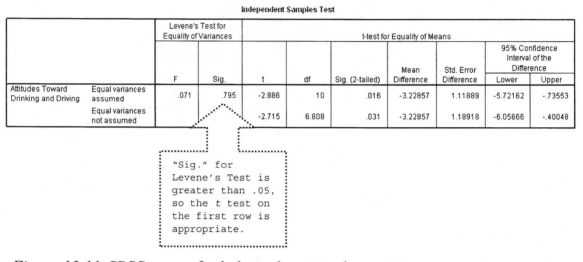

Group Statistics

	Experimental and Control Groups	N	Mean	Std. Deviation	Std. Error Mean
Attitudes Toward Drinking and Driving	Experimental Group	7	10.5714	1.61835	.61168
	Control Group	5	13.8000	2.28035	1.01980

Independent Samples Test

		Levene's Test for Equality of Variances		t-test for Equality of Means						95% Confidence Interval of the Difference	
		F	Sig.	t	df	Sig. (2-tailed)	Mean Difference	Std. Error Difference	Lower	Upper
Attitudes Toward Drinking and Driving	Equal variances assumed	.071	.795	-2.886	10	.016	-3.22857	1.11889	-5.72162	-.73553
	Equal variances not assumed			-2.715	6.808	.031	-3.22857	1.18918	-6.05666	-.40048

"Sig." for Levene's Test is greater than .05, so the *t* test on the first row is appropriate.

Figure 13.11. SPSS output for independent-samples *t* test.

Interpreting and Describing the Results of the Independent-Samples *t* Test

Examine the means in the top box of the output in Figure 13.11 above. The mean of 10.57 for the experimental group indicates that this group has less positive attitudes toward drinking and driving than the control group with a mean of 13.80.

Equality of Variances Assumed

The results of two *t* tests (on the same data) are shown in Figure 13.11 above. In the second box, the *t* test in the top row is based on the assumption that the differences in the variances in the two sets of scores are equal. To determine if this is a valid assumption, examine the "Sig." for "Levene's Test for Equality of Variances." (***See the arrow in Figure 13.11 above.***) The "Sig." is the probability value for Levene's Test. If this "Sig." is greater than .05, it is appropriate to assume equality of variances, and the statistics for the *t* test in the top row should be used. Because "Sig." in Figure 13.11 above (.795) is greater than .05, the *t* test in the top row is the appropriate one to use. Thus, the value of *t* of –2.886 (*not* –2.715) should be reported, as illustrated in Example 13.2 on the next page.

In Figure 13.11 above, the appropriate value of *t* is –2.886 and the associated probability [identified in SPSS as "Sig. (2-tailed)"] is .016. Because .016 is less than .05 (but greater than

.01), the difference between the two means is statistically significant at the .05 level. (See the decision rules in Appendix A to review the guidelines for interpreting probability levels.)

Example 13.2 below shows a statement that could be used in a research report to describe the results shown in Figure 13.11 on the previous page. Note that it starts with reporting the values of the means and standard deviations, which are also provided in Figure 13.11.

Example 13.2

Statement that presents the results of a significant *t* test (equal variances assumed) for the output in Figure 13.11 on the previous page.

"At the end of the experiment, the experimental group had less favorable attitudes toward drinking and driving (*m* = 10.57, *sd* = 1.62) than the control group (*m* = 13.80, *sd* = 2.28). The difference between the two means is statistically significant at the .05 level (*t* = –2.886, *df* = 10)."

Equality of Variances *Not* Assumed

The output in Figure 13.12 on the next page is for a different set of scores than those analyzed above. Notice that the "Sig." for "Levene's Test for Equality of Variances" is .006 (**see the arrow in Figure 13.12 on the next page**). Because .006 is less than .05, it is not appropriate to assume equality of variances, and the values for the *t* test on the second row should be interpreted and reported. Thus, the value of *t* of –3.819 (*not* –3.455) should be reported, as illustrated in Example 13.3 below.

Example 13.3

Statement that presents the results of a significant *t* test (equal variances *not* assumed) for the output in Figure 13.12 on the next page.

"The mean for Group 1 (*m* = 5.80, *sd* = .84) is significantly lower than the mean for Group 2 (*m* = 35.00, *sd* = 18.71) at the .05 level (*t* = –3.82, *df* = 5.02). Because the variances were significantly different, a *t* test that did not assume equality of variances was conducted."

→ T-Test

Group Statistics

	VAR00001	N	Mean	Std. Deviation	Std. Error Mean
VAR00002	1.00	5	5.8000	.83666	.37417
	2.00	6	35.0000	18.70829	7.63763

Independent Samples Test

		Levene's Test for Equality of Variances		t-test for Equality of Means						95% Confidence Interval of the Difference	
		F	Sig.	t	df	Sig. (2-tailed)	Mean Difference	Std. Error Difference		Lower	Upper
VAR00002	Equal variances assumed	12.630	.006	-3.455	9	.007	-29.20000	8.45047		-48.31628	-10.08372
	Equal variances not assumed			-3.819	5.024	.012	-29.20000	7.64679		-48.82849	-9.57151

"Sig." for
Levene's Test is
less than .05, so
the *t* test on
second row is
appropriate.

Figure 13.12. Output for an example in which equality of variance should not be assumed. See Example 13.3 on the previous page.

Exercise for Chapter 13

Analyze the data in Table 13.2 below. The experimental group received instruction in calculus via the Internet while the control group received traditional classroom instruction. The data consist of the number-right scores on the final examination. Conduct an independent-samples *t* test, and then answer the questions that follow.

Table 13.2

Calculus Examination Scores for Experimental and Control Groups

Participant number	Group	Codes for groups	Calculus final examination scores
1	Experimental	1	30
2	Control	2	28
3	Control	2	33
4	Experimental	1	26
5	Experimental	1	34
6	Control	2	34
7	Experimental	1	37
8	Control	2	33
9	Experimental	1	26
10	Control	2	26

a. What is the value of the mean for the experimental group? _____

b. What is the mean for the control group? _____

c. What is the value of *t*? _____

d. What is the associated probability? _____

e. Is the difference between the experimental groups' and control groups' means statistically significant at the .05 level? _____

f. Write a statement of the results of the significance test.

_____

_____

Notes:

Chapter 14

One-Way ANOVA

***Learning objectives*:**

1. Identify the purpose of a one-way ANOVA.

2. Conduct a one-way ANOVA.

3. Interpret the results of a one-way ANOVA in terms of the null hypothesis and statistical significance.

4. Present the results of a one-way ANOVA in a research report.

Purpose of a One-Way ANOVA

In Chapter 13, you learned how to use an independent-samples t test to determine the significance of the difference between two means. A one-way ANOVA can perform the same type of test for a set of *two or more means.*[1]

Table 14.1 below is reproduced from Chapter 7 (it is captioned Table 7.3 on page 77 in that chapter). The data are from an experiment in which participants were assigned at random to receive either high, moderate, or low dosages of a pain-reducing medication. The means represent the reported pain levels for each group. As you can see, the High group reported less pain than the Moderate group, which reported less pain than the Low group. A one-way ANOVA can determine whether the set of differences created by these three means is statistically significant. As with the t test, if it is statistically significant, the null hypothesis is rejected.

Table 14.1

Means and Standard Deviations of Pain Scores for Three Dosage Levels

Dosage level	Mean	Standard deviation
High ($n = 3$)	2.00	1.00
Moderate ($n = 3$)	5.67	2.08
Low ($n = 3$)	7.00	1.00

Note. Pain measured on a scale from 0 (no pain) to 10 (extreme pain). The higher the score, the more pain.

---

[1] Either the t test or ANOVA can be used to test for the difference between two means. For two means, both techniques will yield the same probability that the null hypothesis is correct. ANOVA differs from the t test in that it can also provide probabilities for sets of differences among more than two means.

Conducting a One-Way ANOVA

Step 1: Open the data file that you saved with the name "Dosage and Pain" while working through Chapter 7.

The statistics in Table 14.1 on the previous page are for the data in the file named "Dosage and Pain." If you do not have this file saved, recreate the data file by executing Steps 1 through 10 in Chapter 7, using the data in Table 7.1 on page 69 in that chapter.

Step 2: Click on "Analyze," then move the cursor to "Compare Means," and then click on "One-Way ANOVA...."

See Figure 14.1 below.

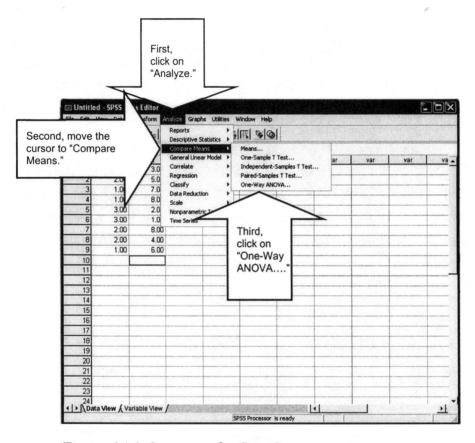

Figure 14.1. Sequence for Step 2.

Step 3: Click on the bottom arrowhead to move "Dosage Level" to the "Factor" box.

By default, the first variable in the list (in this case, "Dosage Level") will already be selected (highlighted in blue) by SPSS. In SPSS, the grouping variable (in this case, the groups formed by the three dosage levels) is called the "Factor."

See Figure 14.2 below.

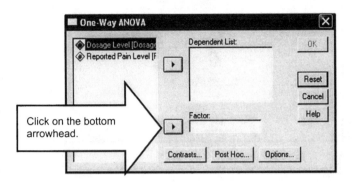

Figure 14.2. Step 3.

Step 4: Click on "Reported Pain Level" to select it, and then click on the top arrowhead to move "Reported Pain Level" to the "Dependent List."

The *dependent variable* is the outcome variable in an experiment. Note that for a one-way ANOVA, the dependent variable should be at the *scale* level of measurement. (See Chapter 1 for a discussion of levels of measurement.)

See Figure 14.3 below.

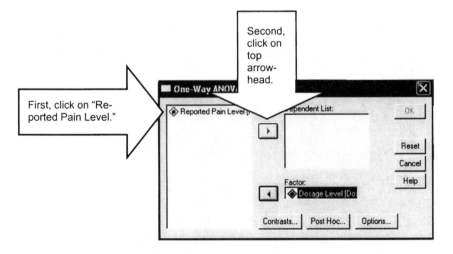

Figure 14.3. Sequence for Step 4.

Step 5: Click on "Options...."

See Figure 14.4 on the next page.

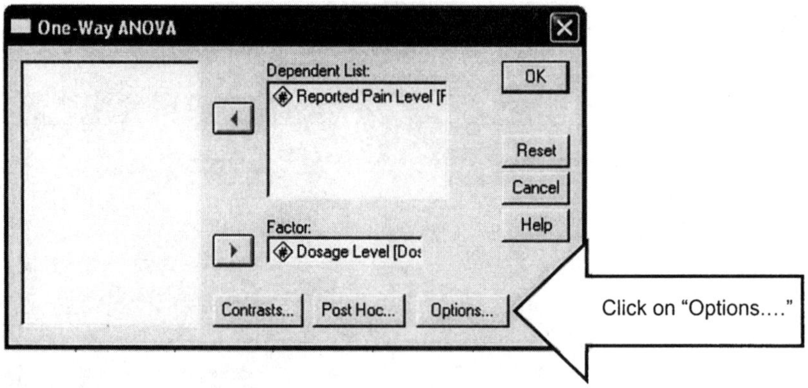

Figure 14.4. Step 5.

Step 6: Click on the box to the left of "Descriptive," and then click on "Continue."

See Figure 14.5 below. After you click on the box, a check mark will appear in it. This tells SPSS to include descriptive statistics such as means and standard deviations in the output.

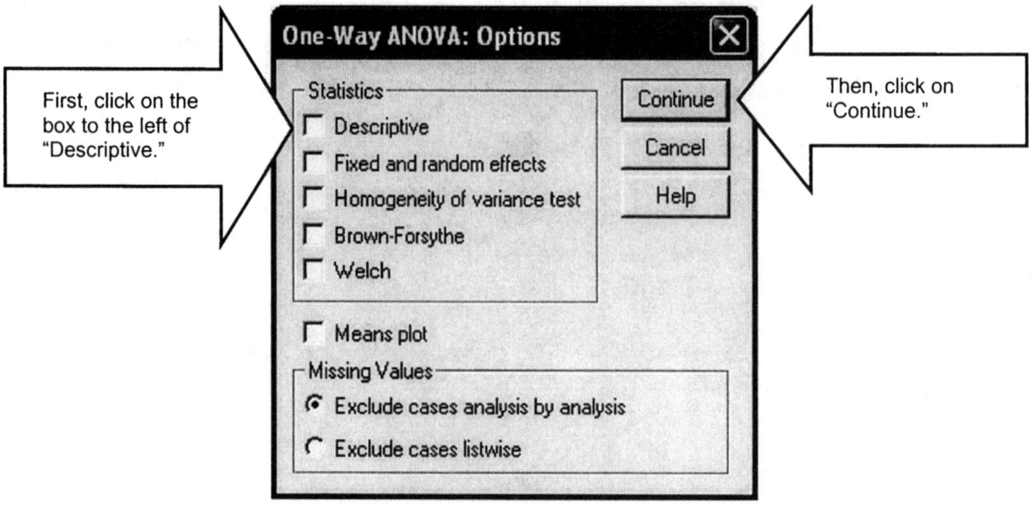

Figure 14.5. Sequence for Step 6.

Step 7: Click OK.

See Figure 14.6 on the next page.

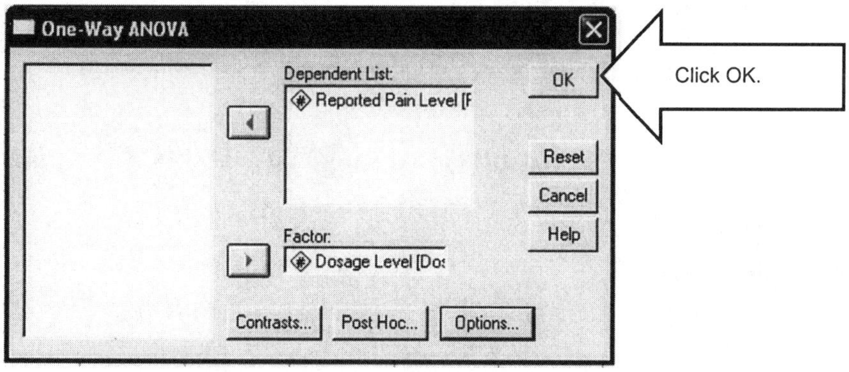

Figure 14.6. Step 7.

After executing Step 7, the output for the one-way ANOVA shown in Figure 14.7 below will appear on the screen.

Oneway

Descriptives

Reported Pain Level

	N	Mean	Std. Deviation	Std. Error	95% Confidence Interval for Mean		Minimum	Maximum
					Lower Bound	Upper Bound		
Low Dosage	3	7.0000	1.00000	.57735	4.5159	9.4841	6.00	8.00
Moderate Dosage	3	5.6667	2.08167	1.20185	.4955	10.8378	4.00	8.00
High Dosage	3	2.0000	1.00000	.57735	-.4841	4.4841	1.00	3.00
Total	9	4.8889	2.57121	.85707	2.9125	6.8653	1.00	8.00

ANOVA

Reported Pain Level

	Sum of Squares	df	Mean Square	F	Sig.
Between Groups	40.222	2	20.111	9.526	.014
Within Groups	12.667	6	2.111		
Total	52.889	8			

Probability = .014

$F = 9.526$

Figure 14.7. SPSS output for one-way ANOVA.

Interpreting the SPSS Output

There are two boxes in the SPSS output in Figure 14.7 above. The top box shows the descriptive statistics, including the means and standard deviations. The bottom box shows the results of the one-way ANOVA, which yields a value of F of 9.526 and the associated probability of .014 (indicated by "Sig." in SPSS). Using the guidelines for determining significance in Appendix A, the differences among the means can be declared to be significant at the .05 level because the probability of .014 is less than .05 (but greater than .01).

Reporting the Results of a One-Way ANOVA in a Research Report

First, report the means and standard deviations. Then, report the value of F, the degrees of freedom, and indicate whether F is statistically significant. Example 14.1 below shows a statement of results.

Example 14.1
Report of the Results of a One-Way ANOVA

"Pain was reported on a scale on which lower scores indicate less pain. For the high dosage group, the mean reported pain level was 2.00 (sd = 1.00). The mean pain levels for the moderate dosage and low dosage groups were 5.67 (sd = 2.08) and 7.00 (sd = 1.00), respectively. The differences among the means are statistically significant at the .05 level [$F(2, 6) = 9.526$]."

In Example 14.1 above, note that an italicized F is used, unlike SPSS, which does not italicize statistical symbols. Also, note that it is traditional to report the degrees of freedom for Between Groups and Within Groups (which are 2 and 6 in the SPSS output in Figure 14.7 on the previous page). In Example 14.1, the degrees of freedom are reported in parentheses immediately following the symbol F.

Exercise for Chapter 14

You will be analyzing the data in Table 14.2 on the next page, which contains estimated hours of Internet usage for samples from three socioeconomic (SES) groups. Execute Steps 1 through 11 in Chapter 7 of this book to enter the data. Name the first variable "SES" and label it "Socioeconomic Status." Use the "Value Labels" of 3 = "High SES," 2 = "Middle SES," and 1 = "Low SES." Name the dependent variable "Internet" and label it "Hours of Internet Usage."

After executing Steps 1 through 11 in Chapter 7, follow Steps 2 through 7 in this chapter to conduct a one-way ANOVA.

Table 14.2

Hours of Daily Internet Usage for Three Socioeconomic Groups

Participant number	SES	Codes for SES levels	Hours of internet usage (weekly)
1	High	3	10
2	High	3	12
3	High	3	11
4	High	3	15
5	Middle	2	14
6	Middle	2	13
7	Middle	2	10
8	Middle	2	12
9	Low	1	9
10	Low	1	11
11	Low	1	8
12	Low	1	12

Conduct a one-way ANOVA, and answer the questions below.

a. What is the value of the mean for the low SES group? _____

b. What is the value of the mean for the middle SES group? _____

c. What is the value of the mean for the high SES group? _____

d. What is the value of *F*? _____

e. What is the value of the associated probability? _____

f. Are the differences among the means for the SES groups statistically significant at the .05 level? _____

g. Write a statement of the results of the significance test.

_____

_____

Notes:

Chapter 15

Chi-Square Goodness of Fit Test

Learning objectives:

1. Identify the purpose of the chi-square goodness of fit test.
2. Conduct a chi-square goodness of fit test.
3. Interpret the results of a chi-square goodness of fit test in terms of the null hypothesis and statistical significance.
4. Present the results of the chi-square goodness of fit test in a research report.

Purpose of the Chi-Square Goodness of Fit Test

The chi-square test is used with *nominal data*. (See Chapter 1 in this book to review types of data.) Example 15.1 below describes a survey in which one nominal variable was measured.[1]

Example 15.1
A survey with one nominal variable.

A researcher drew a random sample of 20 students from a high school class and asked each student to name the candidate for whom he or she planned to vote to become student-body president. Each student named either "John Doe" or "Jane Smith." The raw data are shown in Table 15.1 on the next page. As you can see, 11 students named Smith and 9 named Doe.

Note that in Example 15.1 above the data consist of *names* ("Doe" or "Smith"). Hence, the data are nominal. Although there is an 11 to 9 difference in favor of Smith, a sample of only 20 students was surveyed. Thus, it is possible that there is no true difference in the whole population of seniors. In other words, the difference observed in the sample might not exist in the population. The *null hypothesis* for this example states that "There is no true difference." Thus, the null hypothesis asserts that the population is evenly split and that a difference in the survey was observed only because the sample is not representative of the population.

In Table 15.1 on the next page, the nominal data have been coded as follows: 1 = Smith and 2 = Doe.

---

[1] Two chi-square tests are covered in this book. The chi-square goodness of fit test is covered in this chapter and the chi-square test of independence is covered in Chapter 16.

Table 15.1

Results of a High School Election Poll

Student number	Candidate preferred	Codes for candidates
1	Smith	1
2	Doe	2
3	Smith	1
4	Doe	2
5	Doe	2
6	Smith	1
7	Smith	1
8	Smith	1
9	Doe	2
10	Smith	1
11	Doe	2
12	Smith	1
13	Doe	2
14	Smith	1
15	Smith	1
16	Doe	2
17	Doe	2
18	Smith	1
19	Doe	2
20	Smith	1

Conducting a Chi-Square Goodness of Fit Test

Step 1: Click on "Variable View," then name the variable "Candidate," then click on "Values," and then click on the small gray box that will appear under "Values."

See Figure 15.1 on the next page.

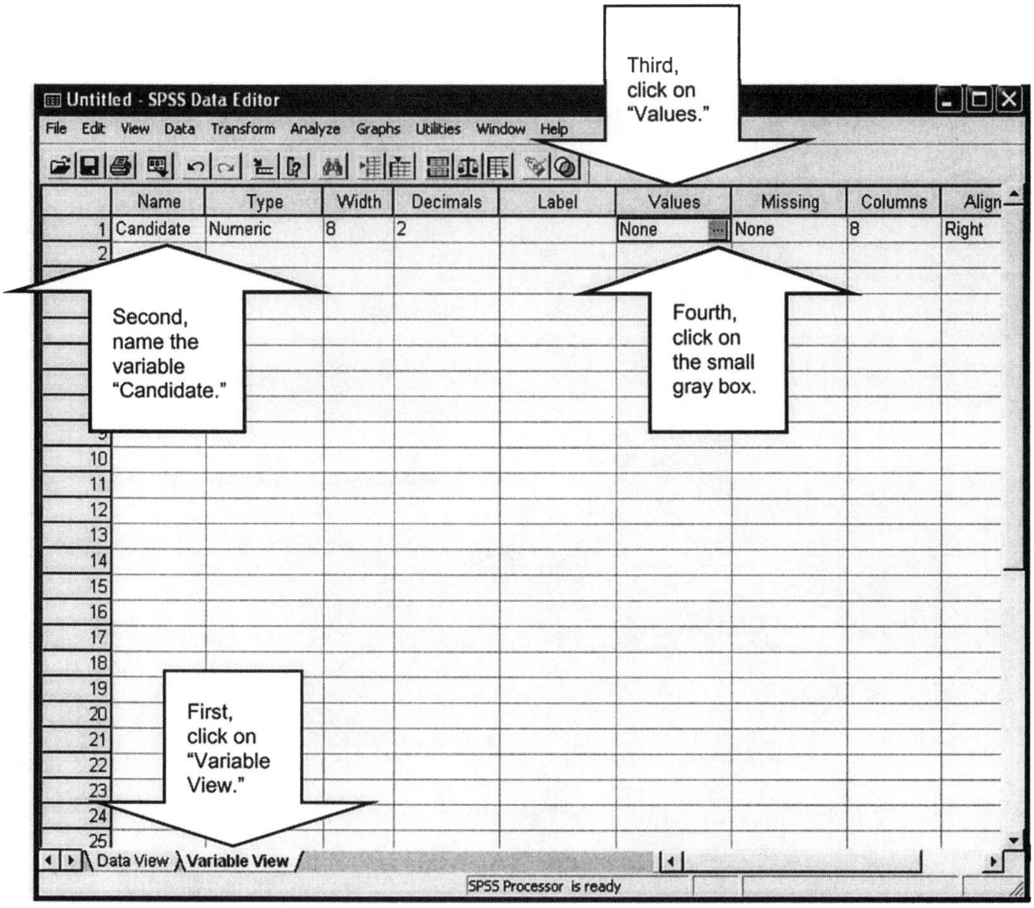

Figure 15.1. Sequence for Step 1.

After executing Step 1, the "Value Labels" dialog box will appear on the screen. In this box, you will be identifying the codes for Smith and Doe in Table 15.1 on the previous page.

Step 2: Type "1" for the "Value," then type "Jane Smith" for the "Value Label," and then click "Add."

Do *not* type quotation marks around the 1 or around Jane Smith's name; SPSS will automatically add them after you click "Add." ***See Figure 15.2 on the next page.***

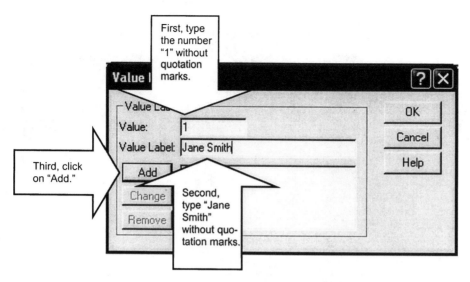

Figure 15.2. Sequence for Step 2.

Step 3: Type "2" for the "Value," then type "John Doe" for the "Value Label," and then click "Add."

Do *not* type quotation marks around the 2 or around John Doe's name; SPSS will automatically add them after you click "Add." ***See the arrows for Step 3 in Figure 15.3 below.***

Step 4: Click OK.

See the arrow for Step 4 in Figure 15.3 below.

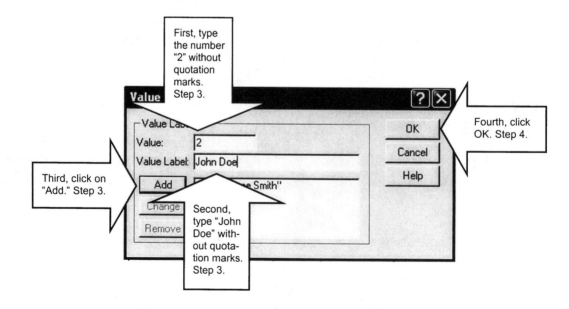

Figure 15.3. Sequence for Steps 3 and 4.

Step 5: Click on "Data View" and enter the codes.

Figure 15.4 below shows the Data View screen after the codes from Table 15.1 on page 156 have been entered.

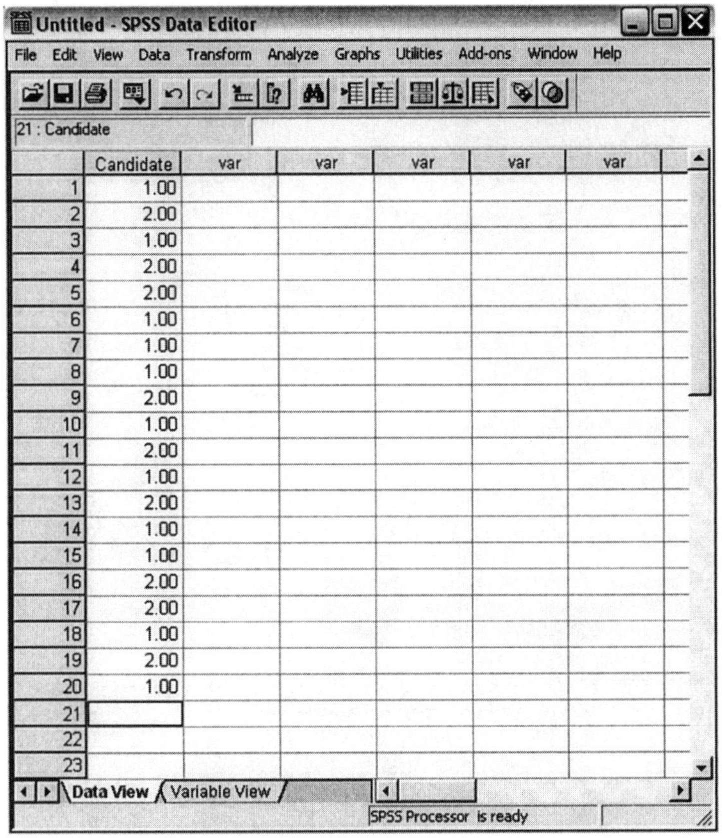

Figure 15.4. Data View screen after the codes for candidates have been entered.

Step 6: Click on "Analyze," then move the cursor to "Nonparametric Tests," and then click on "Chi-Square...."

See Figure 15.5 on the next page.

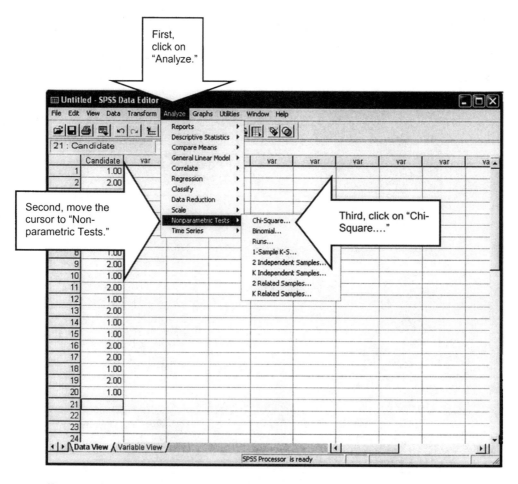

Figure 15.5. Sequence for Step 6.

After executing Step 6, you will see the "Chi-Square Test" dialog box. The variable named "Candidate" will already be selected by SPSS (indicated by being highlighted in blue).

Step 7: Click on arrowhead to move "Candidate" to the "Test Variable List" and click OK.

See Figure 15.6 on the next page.

Note that by default, SPSS has selected "All categories equal." This means that the observed data (11 for Smith and 9 for Doe) will be tested against expected values of 10 and 10 (equal values). Also, note that the null hypothesis discussed earlier in this chapter states that there is no true difference. If there is no true difference, then the frequencies for both candidates should be equal.

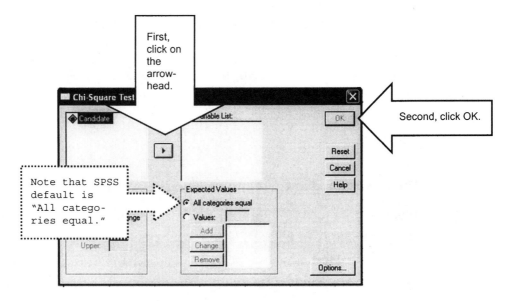

Figure 15.6. Sequence for Step 7.

After executing Step 7, the SPSS output shown in Figure 15.7 below will be shown on the screen.

→ NPar Tests

Chi-Square Test

Frequencies

Candidate

	Observed N	Expected N	Residual
Jane Smith	11	10.0	1.0
John Doe	9	10.0	-1.0
Total	20		

Test Statistics

	Candidate
Chi-Square [a]	.200
df	1
Asymp. Sig.	.655

a. 0 cells (.0%) have expected frequencies less than 5. The minimum expected cell frequency is 10.0.

Figure 15.7. Raw SPSS output for the data in Table 15.1 on page 156.

Interpreting the SPSS Output

The probability the null hypothesis is correct determines whether it should be rejected and statistical significance be declared. In the SPSS output, the probability is indicated by the term "Asymp. Sig." As you can see in Figure 15.7 on the previous page, the probability is .655. According to the guidelines in Appendix A, the value of chi-square is *not* significant because .655 is greater than .05.

Describing the Results of the Chi-Square Goodness of Fit Test in a Research Report

First, report the frequencies for each candidate, which are indicated by the term "Observed N" in the SPSS output in Figure 15.7 on the previous page. Then, describe the results of the chi-square significance test. This is done in Example 15.2 below. Note that the symbol n (and not "N" as used in SPSS) should be used in the research report.[2] Also, note that the symbol for chi-square is χ^2.

Example 15.2
Statement that presents the results of an insignificant chi-square goodness of fit test for the output in Figure 15.7 on the previous page.

"Candidate Smith ($n = 11$) was favored over Candidate Doe ($n = 9$) in the survey. However, the difference was not statistically significant at the .05 level ($\chi^2 = .200$, $df = 1$). Thus, the election is too close to call."

---

[2] Statisticians use a lowercase, italicized n as the symbol for the number of cases in a sample. They use an uppercase, italicized N as a symbol for the number in an entire population.

Exercise for Chapter 15

You will be analyzing the data in Table 15.2 below. Twenty students were surveyed to determine which color they preferred for the pants and skirts of their school uniforms. Conduct a chi-square goodness of fit test to test the null hypothesis that says that there is no true difference in the population from which the sample was drawn.

Table 15.2
Color Preferences for School Uniforms

Student number	Preferred color	Codes for colors
1	Tan	1
2	Blue	2
3	Brown	3
4	Tan	1
5	Tan	1
6	Blue	2
7	Blue	2
8	Blue	2
9	Blue	2
10	Tan	1
11	Blue	2
12	Brown	3
13	Tan	1
14	Blue	2
15	Blue	2
16	Blue	2
17	Blue	2
18	Blue	2
19	Blue	2
20	Brown	3

a. What is the observed value *n* for Tan? _____

b. What is the observed value *n* for Blue? _____

c. What is the observed value *n* for Brown? _____

d. What is the value of chi-square? _____

e. What is the associated probability? _____

f. Are the observed values significantly different at the .05 level from expected values of 6.7 for each color? _____

g. Write a statement of the results of the significance test.

_____

_____

Chapter 16

Chi-Square Test of Independence

Learning objectives:

1. Identify the purpose of the chi-square test of independence.
2. Conduct a chi-square test of independence.
3. Interpret the results of a chi-square test of independence in terms of the null hypothesis and statistical significance.
4. Present the results of the chi-square test of independence in a research report.

Purpose of the Chi-Square Test of Independence

The *chi-square test of independence* is used to test for the statistical significance of the relationship between two *nominal variables*. (See Chapter 1 to review types of variables.) Example 16.1 below describes a survey in which two nominal variables were measured.[1]

Example 16.1
A survey with two nominal variables.

A researcher drew a random sample of 24 registered voters and asked whether they planned to vote for Proposition A. (How they planned to vote, either "yes" or "no," is a nominal variable.) The researcher also asked them to name their gender. (What they name, either "male" or "female," is also a nominal variable.) The researcher obtained these results:

	Yes	No
Male	8	4
Female	5	7

The researcher observed that men were more likely to vote "yes," while women were more likely to vote "no." Because only a sample was questioned in the survey, a chi-square test of independence is needed in order to determine whether the apparent relationship between gender and voting behavior is statistically significant. The null hypothesis states that there is no true relationship between gender and voting behavior.

---

[1] Two chi-square tests are covered in this book. The chi-square goodness of fit test was covered in the previous chapter.

Table 16.1 below shows the nominal data for the two variables described in Example 16.1 on the previous page.

Table 16.1

Results of a High School Election Poll

Voter number	Gender	Codes for gender	Plan to vote for Prop. A?	Codes for voting
1	Male	1	Yes	1
2	Male	1	Yes	1
3	Male	1	Yes	1
4	Male	1	Yes	1
5	Male	1	Yes	1
6	Male	1	Yes	1
7	Male	1	Yes	1
8	Male	1	Yes	1
9	Male	1	No	2
10	Male	1	No	2
11	Male	1	No	2
12	Male	1	No	2
13	Female	2	Yes	1
14	Female	2	Yes	1
15	Female	2	Yes	1
16	Female	2	Yes	1
17	Female	2	Yes	1
18	Female	2	No	2
19	Female	2	No	2
20	Female	2	No	2
21	Female	2	No	2
22	Female	2	No	2
23	Female	2	No	2
24	Female	2	No	2

Conducting a Chi-Square Test of Independence

Step 1: Click on "Variable View," name the first variable "Gender," click on the first cell under "Values," then click on the small gray box that will appear under "Values."

See Figure 16.1 on the next page.

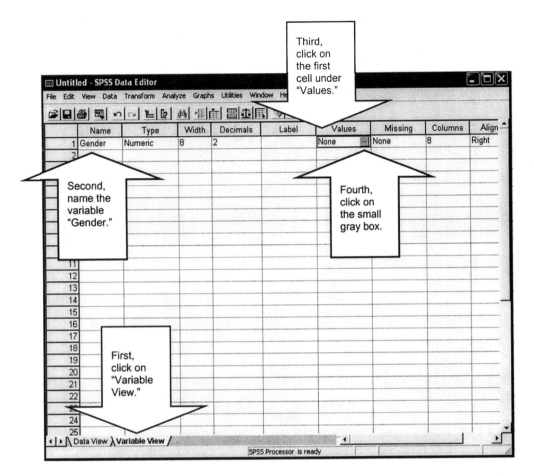

Figure 16.1. Sequence for Step 1.

After executing Step 1, the "Value Labels" dialog box will appear on the screen.

Step 2: In the "Value Labels" dialog box, type "1" for the "Value," and type "Male" for the "Value Label," and then click "Add."

Do *not* type quotation marks around the 1 or around Male; SPSS will automatically add them after you click "Add." ***See Figure 16.2 on the next page.***

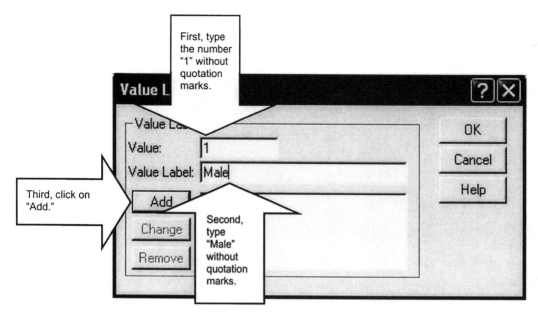

Figure 16.2. Sequence for Step 2.

Step 3: In the "Value Labels" dialog box, type "2" for the "Value," and type "Female" for the "Value Label," then click "Add," and then click OK.

Do *not* type quotation marks around the 2 or around Female; SPSS will automatically add them after you click "Add." ***See Figure 16.3 below.***

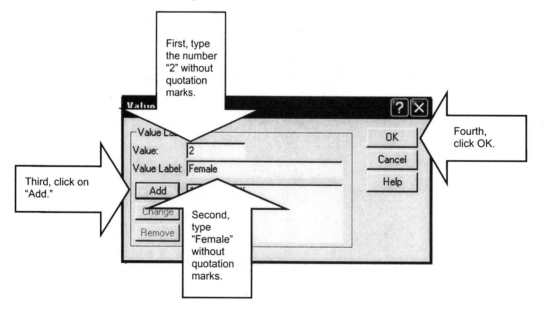

Figure 16.3. Sequence for Step 3.

Step 4: While still in "Variable View," name the second variable "Vote," click on the second cell under "Values," then click on the small gray box that will appear under "Values."

See Figure 16.4 below.

After executing Step 4, the "Value Labels" dialog box will appear again on the screen.

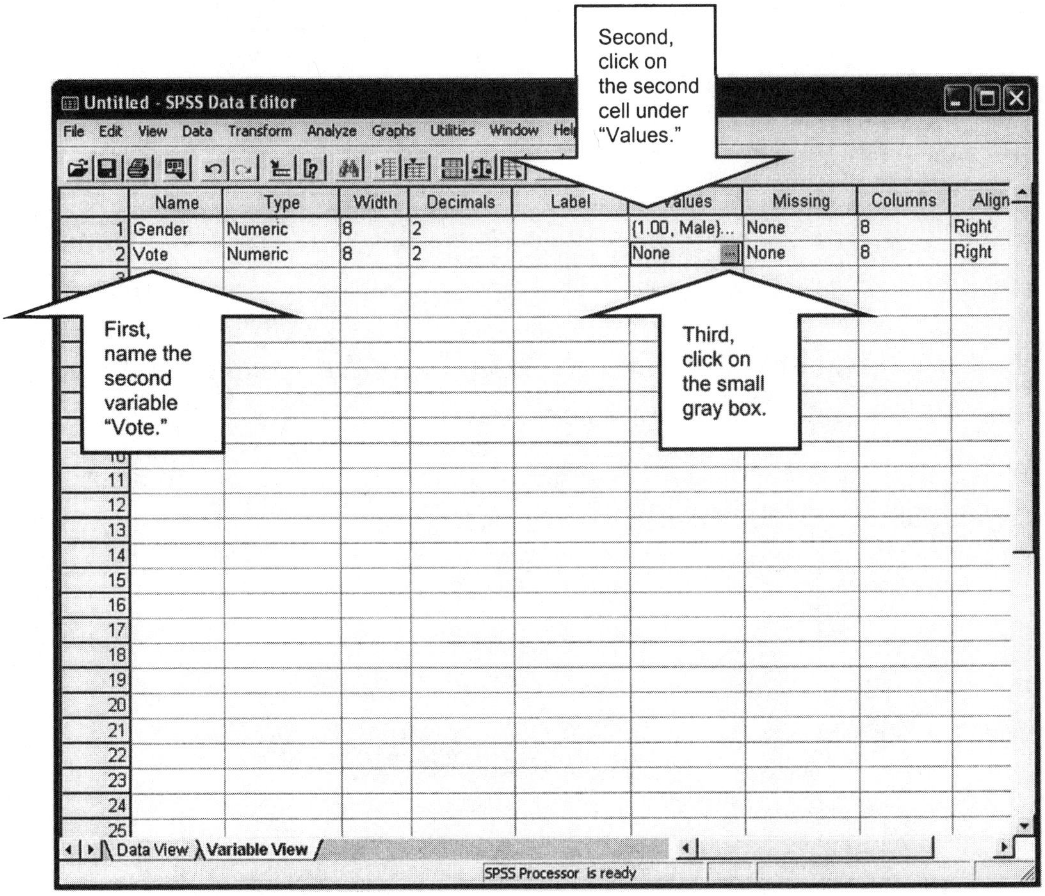

Second, click on the second cell under "Values."

First, name the second variable "Vote."

Third, click on the small gray box.

	Name	Type	Width	Decimals	Label	Values	Missing	Columns	Align
1	Gender	Numeric	8	2		{1.00, Male}...	None	8	Right
2	Vote	Numeric	8	2		None	None	8	Right

Figure 16.4. Sequence for Step 4.

Step 5: In the "Value Labels" dialog box, type "1" for the "Value," and type "Yes" for the "Value Label," and then click "Add."

Do *not* type quotation marks around the 1 or around Yes; SPSS will automatically add them after you click "Add." ***See Figure 16.5 on the next page.***

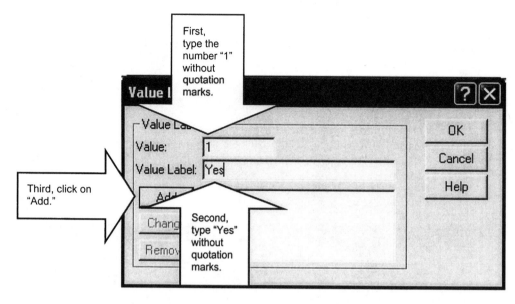

Figure 16.5. Sequence for Step 5.

Step 6: In the "Value Labels" dialog box, type "2" for the "Value," and type "No" for the "Value Label," and then click "Add."

Do *not* type quotation marks around the 2 or around No; SPSS will automatically add them after you click "Add." ***See Figure 16.6 below.***

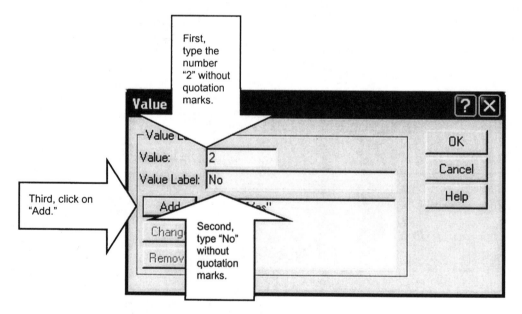

Figure 16.6. Sequence for Step 6.

Step 7: In the "Value Labels" dialog box, click OK.

See Figure 16.7 below.

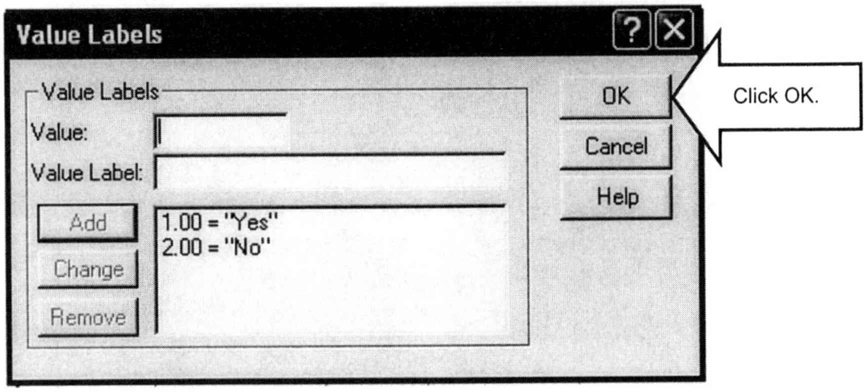

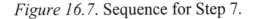

Figure 16.7. Sequence for Step 7.

Step 8: Click on the "Data View" tab, and then enter the codes for "Gender" and "Vote."

The codes are shown in Table 16.1 on page 166. *Figure 16.8 below* shows the Data View screen after the codes have been entered.

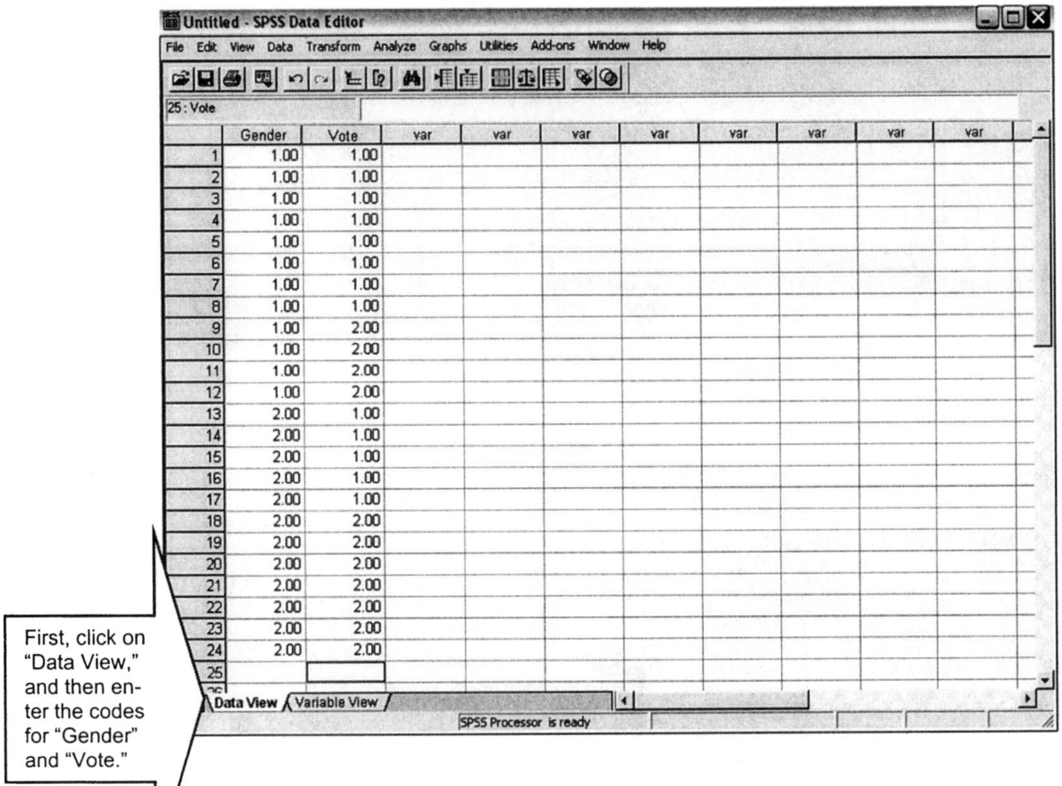

	Gender	Vote
1	1.00	1.00
2	1.00	1.00
3	1.00	1.00
4	1.00	1.00
5	1.00	1.00
6	1.00	1.00
7	1.00	1.00
8	1.00	1.00
9	1.00	2.00
10	1.00	2.00
11	1.00	2.00
12	1.00	2.00
13	2.00	1.00
14	2.00	1.00
15	2.00	1.00
16	2.00	1.00
17	2.00	1.00
18	2.00	2.00
19	2.00	2.00
20	2.00	2.00
21	2.00	2.00
22	2.00	2.00
23	2.00	2.00
24	2.00	2.00

First, click on "Data View," and then enter the codes for "Gender" and "Vote."

Figure 16.8. Codes for "Gender" and "Vote" have been entered in Data View. Step 8.

Step 9: Click on "Analyze," then move the cursor to "Descriptive Statistics," and then click on "Crosstabs...."

See Figure 16.9 below.

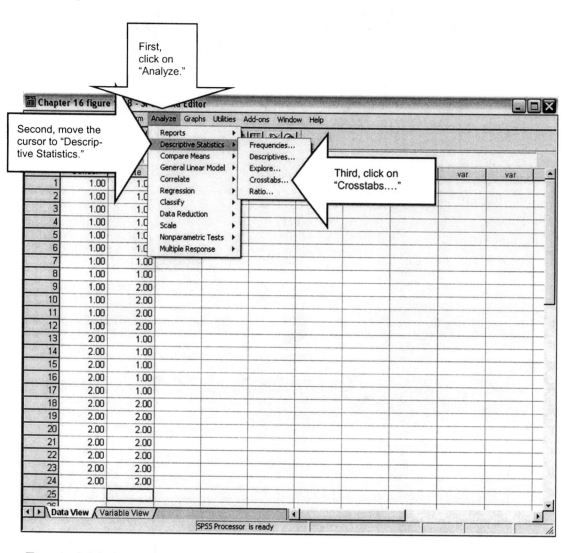

Figure 16.9. Sequence for Step 9.

Step 10: Click on the top arrowhead to move "Gender" to the "Rows" box.

See Figure 16.10 on the next page.

Note that by default, SPSS has selected and highlighted in blue the first variable in the list (Gender). Clicking on the top arrowhead moves "Gender" so that it will be presented in the rows in the SPSS output.

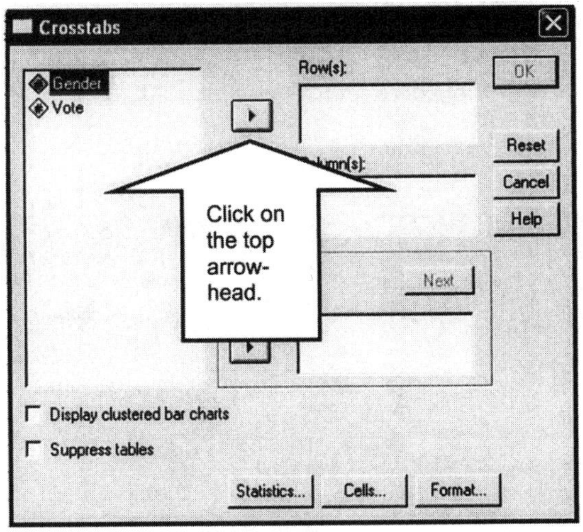

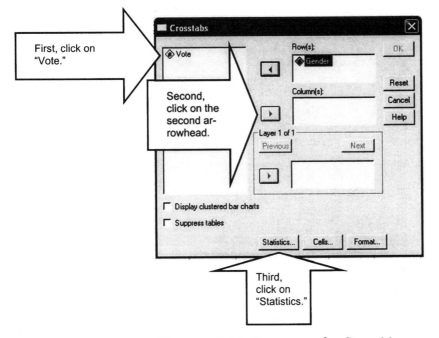

Figure 16.10. Step 10.

Step 11: Click on "Vote" to select it, then click on the second arrowhead to move "Vote" to the "Columns" box, and then click on "Statistics."

See Figure 16.11 below.

Note that this step tells SPSS to present the votes (yes or no) in the columns of the output.

Figure 16.11. Sequence for Step 11.

Step 12: Click on the box to the left of "Chi-square," and then click on "Continue."

After you click on the box, a check mark will appear in it. *See Figure 16.12 below.*

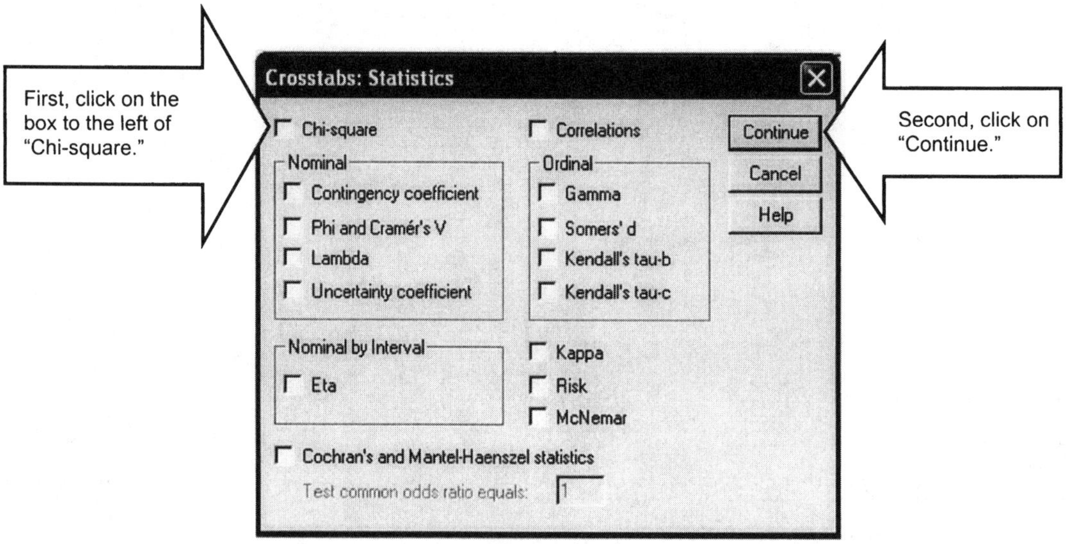

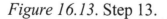

Figure 16.12. Sequence for Step 12.

Step 13: Click on OK.

See Figure 16.13 below.

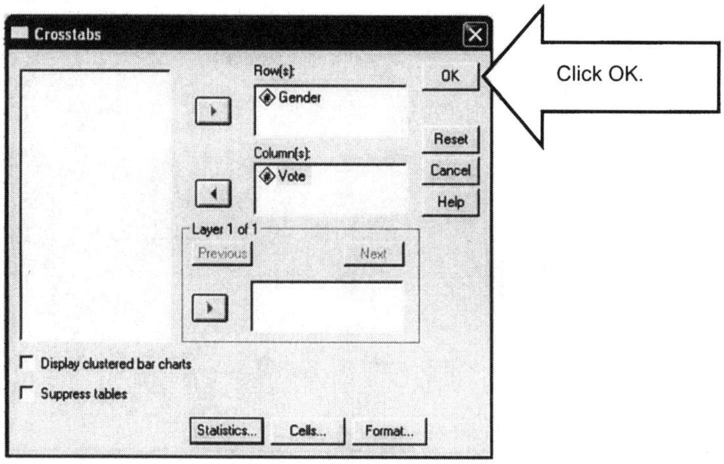

Figure 16.13. Step 13.

After you execute Step 13, the SPSS output will appear on the screen. *See Figure 16.14 on the next page.*

➜ Crosstabs

Case Processing Summary

	Cases					
	Valid		Missing		Total	
	N	Percent	N	Percent	N	Percent
Gender * Vote	24	100.0%	0	.0%	24	100.0%

Gender * Vote Crosstabulation

Count

		Vote		Total
		Yes	No	
Gender	Male	8	4	12
	Female	5	7	12
Total		13	11	24

Chi-Square Tests

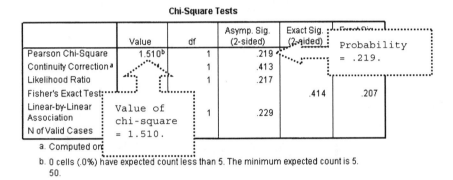

	Value	df	Asymp. Sig. (2-sided)	Exact Sig. (2-sided)	Exact Sig. (1-sided)
Pearson Chi-Square	1.510[b]	1	.219		
Continuity Correction[a]		1	.413		
Likelihood Ratio		1	.217		
Fisher's Exact Test				.414	.207
Linear-by-Linear Association		1	.229		
N of Valid Cases					

Probability = .219.

Value of chi-square = 1.510.

a. Computed on

b. 0 cells (.0%) have expected count less than 5. The minimum expected count is 5.50.

Figure 16.14. SPSS output for chi-square test of independence.

Interpreting the SPSS Output

The probability that the null hypothesis is correct determines whether it should be rejected and statistical significance be declared. In the SPSS output, the probability is indicated by the term "Asymp. Sig." As you can see in Figure 16.14 above, the probability is .219. According to the guidelines in Appendix A, the value of chi-square is *not* significant because .219 is greater than .05. Thus, the two variables ("Gender" and "Vote") are independent of each other.

Describing the Results of the Chi-Square Test of Independence in a Research Report

First, report the frequencies for each category on each variable in a table. This is called the "Gender Vote Crosstabulation" in the SPSS output. (The cross tabulations are shown in the second box in the output in Figure 16.14 above.) Then, state whether the results are statistically significant, followed by the value of chi-square (called the "Pearson Chi-Square" in the SPSS output) and the degrees of freedom ("df"). Example 16.2 on the next page illustrates how to do this. Note that the symbol for chi-square is χ^2.

Example 16.2

Statement that presents the results of an insignificant chi-square test of independence for the output in Figure 16.14 on the previous page.

"Males were more likely to vote 'Yes,' while females were more likely to vote 'No,' as shown in Table 16.2.[2] However, the relationship between gender and voting was not statistically significant at the .05 level ($\chi^2 = 1.510$, $df = 1$). Thus, gender and voting are independent of each other."

Table 16.2

Cross Tabulations for Example 16.1 on Page 165 (see the row data in Table 16.1 on page 166)

	Planned Vote		
	Yes	No	Total
Gender			
Male	8	4	12
Female	5	7	12
Total	13	11	24

Exercise for Chapter 16

You will be analyzing the data in Table 16.3 on the next page. Twenty high school math teachers were surveyed to determine whether they approved of a proposed new mathematics curriculum. The 20 teachers were classified as either experienced or inexperienced teachers. Conduct a chi-square test of independence to test between "approval" and "experience."

In the Variable View mode, name the first variable "Experience," and use the value labels of 1 = Experienced and 2 = Inexperienced. Name the second variable "Approval," and use value labels of 1 = Approve and 2 = Disapprove.

In Step 10, move "Experience" to the "Rows" box. In Step 11, move "Approval" to the "Columns" box.

---

[2] The cross tabulation table in the SPSS output in Figure 16.14 on the previous page has been formatted in Example 16.2 above to be consistent with the style suggested in the *Publication Manual of the American Psychological Association.*

Table 16.3

Results of a Survey of Teachers on a Proposed New Mathematics Curriculum and Teachers' Experience in Teaching

Voter number	Teaching experience	Codes for experience	Approve of curriculum?	Codes for approval
1	Experienced	1	Approve	1
2	Experienced	1	Approve	1
3	Experienced	1	Approve	1
4	Experienced	1	Approve	1
5	Experienced	1	Approve	1
6	Experienced	1	Approve	1
7	Experienced	1	Approve	1
8	Experienced	1	Disapprove	2
9	Experienced	1	Disapprove	2
10	Experienced	1	Disapprove	2
11	Inexperienced	2	Approve	1
12	Inexperienced	2	Approve	1
13	Inexperienced	2	Approve	1
14	Inexperienced	2	Disapprove	2
15	Inexperienced	2	Disapprove	2
16	Inexperienced	2	Disapprove	2
17	Inexperienced	2	Disapprove	2
18	Inexperienced	2	Disapprove	2
19	Inexperienced	2	Disapprove	2
20	Inexperienced	2	Disapprove	2

a. How many of the experienced teachers approved? _____

b. How many of the inexperienced teachers approved? _____

c. What is the value of chi-square? _____

d. What is the associated probability? _____

e. Are the results statistically significant at the .05 level? _____

f. Write a statement of the results of the significance test.

_____

_____

Notes:

Appendix A

Decision Rules for Declaring Statistical Significance

The following are the decision rules for declaring statistical significance at various probability levels. Note that if there is a statistically significant difference, the null hypothesis is rejected. If a test is *not* significant, the null hypothesis is *not* rejected.

a. If the probability displayed by SPSS is equal to or less than .001, reject the null hypothesis and declare the difference to be statistically significant at the .001 level.

b. If the probability displayed by SPSS is equal to or less than .01 (but greater than .001), reject the null hypothesis and declare the difference to be statistically significant at the .01 level.

c. If the probability displayed by SPSS is less than .05 (but greater than .01), reject the null hypothesis and declare the difference to be statistically significant at the .05 level.

d. If the probability displayed by SPSS is equal to .05, reject the null hypothesis and declare the difference to be statistically significant at the .05 level.

e. If the probability displayed by SPSS is *greater* than .05, do *not* reject the null hypothesis and do *not* declare the difference to be statistically significant (i.e., declare it to be statistically *in*significant) at the .05 level.

Table A.1 below shows examples of probability levels and the application of the decision rules.

Table A.1

Examples of the Application of the Decision Rules

If SPSS displays:	Make this decision about the null hypothesis:	Make this declaration:	Notes:
.000	Reject at .001 level.	Statistically significant at the .001 level.	Note that .000 is less than .001.
.003	Reject at .01 level.	Statistically significant at the .01 level.	Note that .003 is less than .01 but greater than .001.
.040	Reject at .05 level.	Statistically significant at the .05 level.	Note that .040 is less than .05 but greater than .01.
.050	Reject at .05 level.	Statistically significant at the .05 level.	Note that .050 is equal to .05.
.070	Do *not* reject at .05 level.	*Not* statistically significant at the .05 level.	Note that .070 is *greater than* .05.

Notes:

Appendix B

Guide to the Information Boxes

Notes:

Notes:

Notes:

Notes: